MAKE YOUR OWN
CALIFORNIA
WILL

Douglas E. Godbe
Attorney at Law

SPHINX® PUBLISHING
AN IMPRINT OF SOURCEBOOKS, INC.®
NAPERVILLE, ILLINOIS
www.SphinxLegal.com

First Edition, 2003

Published by: Sphinx® Publishing, An Imprint of Sourcebooks, Inc.®

Naperville Office
P.O. Box 4410
Naperville, Illinois 60567-4410
630-961-3900
Fax: 630-961-2168
www.sourcebooks.com
www.SphinxLegal.com

This publication is designed to provide accurate and authoritative information in regard to the subject matter covered. It is sold with the understanding that the publisher is not engaged in rendering legal, accounting, or other professional service. If legal advice or other expert assistance is required, the services of a competent professional person should be sought.

From a Declaration of Principles Jointly Adopted by a Committee of the American Bar Association and a Committee of Publishers and Associations

This product is not a substitute for legal advice.

Disclaimer required by Texas statutes.

Library of Congress Cataloging-in-Publication Data
Godbe, Douglas, 1951–
    Make your own California will / by Douglass E. Godbe.-- 1st ed.
          p. cm.
Includes index.
    ISBN 1-57248-246-X (pbk.)
  1. Wills--California--Popular works. 2. Inheritance and
succession--California--Popular works. I. Title.
    KFC201.Z9 G63 2002
    346.79405'4--dc21
                                                            2002012180

Printed and bound in the United States of America.

VHG Paperback — 10 9 8 7 6 5 4 3 2 1

CONTENTS

USING SELF-HELP LAW BOOKS

Before using a self-help law book, you should realize the advantages and disadvantages of doing your own legal work and understand the challenges and diligence that this requires.

THE GROWING TREND

Rest assured that you won't be the first or only person handling your own legal matter. For example, in some states, more than seventy-five percent of divorces and other cases have at least one party representing him or herself. Because of the high cost of legal services, this is a major trend and many courts are struggling to make it easier for people to represent themselves. However, some courts are not happy with people who do not use attorneys and refuse to help them in any way. For some, the attitude is, "Go to the law library and figure it out for yourself."

We at Sphinx write and publish self-help law books to give people an alternative to the often complicated and confusing legal books found in most law libraries. We have made the explanations of the law as simple and easy to understand as possible. Of course, unlike an attorney advising an individual client, we cannot cover every conceivable possibility.

COST/VALUE ANALYSIS

Whenever you shop for a product or service, you are faced with various levels of quality and price. In deciding what product or service to buy, you make a cost/value analysis on the basis of your willingness to pay and the quality you desire.

When buying a car, you decide whether you want transportation, comfort, status, or sex appeal. Accordingly, you decide among such choices as a Neon, a Lincoln, a Rolls Royce, or a Porsche. Before making a decision, you usually weigh the merits of each option against the cost.

When you get a headache, you can take a pain reliever (such as aspirin) or visit a medical specialist for a neurological examination. Given this choice, most people, of course, take a pain reliever, since it costs only pennies; whereas a medical examination costs hundreds of dollars and takes a lot of time. This is usually a logical choice because it is rare to need anything more than a pain reliever for a headache. But in some cases, a headache may indicate a brain tumor and failing to see a specialist right away can result in complications. Should everyone with a headache go to a specialist? Of course not, but people treating their own illnesses must realize that they are betting on the basis of their cost/value analysis of the situation. They are taking the most logical option.

The same cost/value analysis must be made when deciding to do one's own legal work. Many legal situations are very straight forward, requiring a simple form and no complicated analysis. Anyone with a little intelligence and a book of instructions can handle the matter without outside help.

But there is always the chance that complications are involved that only an attorney would notice. To simplify the law into a book like this, several legal cases often must be condensed into a single sentence or paragraph. Otherwise, the book would be several hundred pages long and too complicated for most people. However, this simplification necessarily leaves out many details and nuances that would apply to special or unusual situations. Also, there are many ways to interpret most legal questions. Your case may come before a judge who disagrees with the analysis of our authors.

Therefore, in deciding to use a self-help law book and to do your own legal work, you must realize that you are making a cost/value analysis. You have decided that the money you will save in doing it yourself outweighs the chance that your case will not turn out to your satisfaction. Most people handling their own simple legal matters never have a problem, but occasionally people find that it ended up costing them more to have an attorney straighten out the situation than it would have if they had hired an attorney in the beginning. Keep this in mind if you decide to handle your own case, and be sure to consult an attorney if you feel you might need further guidance.

LOCAL RULES The next thing to remember is that a book that covers the law for the entire nation, or even for an entire state, cannot possibly include every procedural difference of every county court. Whenever possible, we provide the exact form needed; however, in some areas, each county, or even each judge, may require unique forms and procedures. In our *state* books, our forms usually cover the majority of counties in the state, or provide examples of the type of form that will be required. In our *national* books, our forms are sometimes even more general in nature but are designed to give a good idea of the type of form that will be needed in most locations. Nonetheless, keep in mind that your *state*, county, or judge may have a requirement, or use a form, that is not included in this book.

You should not necessarily expect to be able to get all of the information and resources you need solely from within the pages of this book. This book will serve as your guide, giving you specific information whenever possible and helping you to find out what else you will need to know. This is just like if you decided to build your own backyard deck. You might purchase a book on how to build decks. However, such a book would not include the building codes and permit requirements of every city, town, county, and township in the nation; nor would it include the lumber, nails, saws, hammers, and other materials and tools you would need to actually build the deck. You would use the book as your guide, and then do some work and research involving such matters as whether you need a permit of some kind, what type and grade of wood are available in your area, whether to use hand tools or power tools, and how to use those tools.

Before using the forms in a book like this, you should check with your court clerk to see if there are any local rules of which you should be aware, or local forms you will need to use. Often, such forms will require the same information as the forms in the book but are merely laid out differently, use slightly different language, or use different color paper so the clerks can easily find them. They will sometimes require additional information.

CHANGES IN
THE LAW

Besides being subject to state and local rules and practices, the law is subject to change at any time. The courts and the legislatures of all fifty states are constantly revising the laws. It is possible that while you are reading this book, some aspect of the law is being changed or a court is interpreting a law in a different way. You should always check the most recent statutes, rules and regulations to see what, if any changes have been made.

In most cases, the change will be of minimal significance. A form will be redesigned, additional information will be required, or a waiting period will be extended. As a result, you might need to revise a form, file an extra form, or wait out a longer time period; these types of changes will not usually affect the outcome of your case. On the other hand, sometimes a major part of the law is changed, the entire law in a particular area is rewritten, or a case that was the basis of a central legal point is overruled. In such instances, your entire ability to pursue your case may be impaired.

Again, you should weigh the value of your case against the cost of an attorney and make a decision as to what you believe is in your best interest.

INTRODUCTION

The purpose of this book is to:

- describe basic law regarding the disposition of assets with a will;

- guide the reader through the preparation and execution of a will and nomination of guardian;

- advise when a lawyer is needed;

- describe types of property which pass at death without a will; and,

- provide blank forms and samples of completed forms for wills and nomination of guardian, to fit most family situations and estate disposition objectives.

Reading the book and following the instructions will enable you to prepare and execute a will and a nomination of guardian. This book also helps you decide when you need to hire an attorney. After reviewing this book, you might decide to consult with an attorney either to draft your estate plan or to review the will you have prepared from the forms included in this book. In that event, this book will assist you in determining what your estate planning objectives are and to better understand the process when guided by an attorney.

Some estate planners call a will the "wastebasket" of estate planning because, contrary to popular belief, very few assets are disposed of at death under a will. This book will identify what types of property ownership avoids both disposition under a will and probate through the court.

This book will explain the various methods of leaving your assets to your spouse, your adult and minor children, and your friends, including outright bequests, life estates, custodianships, and trusts created under a will.

This book will discuss federal estate taxes and inheritance taxes, however it does not explain how to use a will to minimize or even completely avoid those death taxes. That type of discussion is beyond the scope of this book. If you are interested in this type of detail, please consult and attorney or financial planner.

This book provides forms for more than seventeen different wills, one codicil, and forms for two different nomination of guardians. Sample "filled-in" forms and step-by-step instructions will assist you in completing the forms that best fit your situation and desires. The will forms included with this book cover four family situations: married with children; married without children; unmarried with children; and, unmarried without children. Separate forms are provided for the nomination of guardians for minor children. Finally, an Asset Roadmap "form" is provided which will help you identify your assets both for your own estate planning decisions and to assist the person you appoint to manage your estate after your death.

Chapter 1 is a general section that will familiarize you with various terms and concepts in planning your will. It also generally covers estate and inheritance taxes. Chapter 2 explains what types of assets are subject to disposition under a will and what types of assets can be distributed at death without a will.

Chapter 3 discusses who can be listed as beneficiaries and, as such, who can inherit. Issues related to adult beneficiaries versus beneficiaries who are under the age of 18 and persons who are "disqualified" to inherit due to relationship to the testator are also discussed.

Chapter 4 discusses the various types of bequests that can be made. It explains the advantages and disadvantages of outright bequests, bequests for the lifetime use of the beneficiary (life estates), bequests for minors (custodianships and trusts instead of guardianships), and bequests in trust for a beneficiary's lifetime. Chapter 5 discusses how to select an executor to probate your will and administer your estate, a trustee to manage assets for the benefit of beneficiaries when an outright bequest is not appropriate, and a guardian to care for your orphaned children.

Chapter 6 discusses the formalities necessary to properly execute your will, while Chapter 7 discusses the legal requirements necessary to properly execute an amendment to your will. Chapter 8 discusses how to be sure your will is preserved during your lifetime and not destroyed after your death. Chapter 9 explains the formalities required to revoke a will.

Chapter 10 details the various paragraphs of the will, including the *introductory paragraph*, the *declaration of family status*, the *disposition of assets*, and the *nomination of executors*, as well as the "boilerplate" provisions.

At the end of this book you will find a Glossary of the terms used throughout this title. Appendix A contains various California statutes discussed in this book. Appendix B provides an Asset Roadmap form to list your property for your executor and family. Appendix C provides step-by-step instructions to complete and execute all of the blank forms plus several sample "complete" forms. Appendix D contains more than fifteen "fill-in-the-blank" will forms and two nomination of guardian forms.

AN OVERVIEW   1

WHAT IS A WILL?

A *will* is a written document that disposes of a person's property effective at the death of that person. To be valid, a will must be signed by the person, called the *testator*, whose property it affects.

WHAT IS PROBATE?

Probate is the court supervision of the distribution of the *assets* of a deceased person to his or her *beneficiaries* or *heirs*. Probate exists because there is no other way to change the *title* to assets from the deceased person to the persons entitled under his or her will or, if there is no will, his or her heirs.

Most property never goes through the probate process due to the many exceptions to probate. Assets that do not pass through probate include:

- assets held in *joint tenancy*;

- life insurance proceeds (unless the *estate* is the named beneficiary);

- assets bequeathed in a will outright to a surviving spouse;

- assets that pass to the surviving spouse by *intestate succession*;

- IRAs, 401(k)s and pensions (unless the estate is the beneficiary);

- *totten trust* bank accounts, *transfer on death* brokerage accounts and *payable on death* savings bonds or bank accounts;

- assets held in a *trust*; and,

- assets that are otherwise eligible for probate but total under $100,000.

FINDING THE LAW

The law itself is found primarily in the California Probate Code. The California Probate Code contains all of the statutes (called *code sections*) relating to wills, probate, and the probate process. The California Probate Code can be purchased in most law bookstores for about $25 and is also available at several Internet websites such as:

www.leginfo.ca.gov/calaw.html

COMMUNITY AND SEPARATE PROPERTY

The title to property usually does not state whether it is *community* or *separate*. Even when the title has only the name of one spouse or says "separate property", it may still be community property. If a property owner is married, the only way to determine whether it is separate or community property is by written agreement between the spouses or court determination. You may dispose of all of your separate property at your death, but only your one-half interest in community property.

SEPARATE PROPERTY   In California, property is either separate property or community property. Separate property are all assets of a single, divorced, or widowed person. It can also be the assets of a married person which were acquired before marriage or after marriage by gift or inheritance.

COMMUNITY PROPERTY   Community property (defined in the California Probate Code Section 28) is property acquired during marriage by a married person, unless acquired by gift or inheritance. When a married person living in California acquires property, either *real property* situated in California or *personal property* situated anywhere, the law assumes it is acquired by the "community." This means each spouse owns half the property, even if the title to the property is in the name of only one of the spouses. The couple may, however, by agreement (in writing if the agreement is after 1985), make the property the separate property of one spouse or the other.

Another aspect of community property is that each spouse may transfer, at his or her death, his or her one-half interest in any community property asset to someone other than the surviving spouse. If that transfer by one spouse at death to someone *other than* his or her surviving spouse is by will, a probate is likely to be required. The surviving spouse's one-half interest in the community property, regardless of the disposition made by the predeceased spouse, is not probated.

Community property can only exist during the marriage. At the moment of the death of either spouse, the property then becomes separate property—one-half owned by the deceased spouse and one-half owned by the surviving spouse. Any property inherited from the deceased spouse by the surviving spouse becomes the separate property of the surviving spouse.

QUASI-
COMMUNITY
PROPERTY

Quasi-community property is property acquired by a married person living outside California that would have been community property if the person were living in California. Read the exact definition carefully. It applies to all personal property situated anywhere and all real property situated in California. (For a more detailed definition, refer to California Probate Code Section 66.)

ASSETS

As a simple guideline, all assets of the deceased must go through probate unless the law specifically provides otherwise. However, most property that belonged to a deceased person does not go through probate because the exceptions to probate are numerous.

Assets that do not have to be probated are:

- those where the title lists the *decedent* (deceased person) and at least one living person as *joint tenants*;

- those passing outright to a surviving spouse (this does not include property passing to a trust for the benefit of a surviving spouse);

- bank accounts where the title is in the decedent's name "as trustee for" or "in trust for" a living person;

- brokerage accounts where the title is in the decedent's name with the designation "transfer on death" to a living person;

- bank accounts or savings bonds where the title is in the name of the decedent with the instruction to "pay on death" to a living person;

- assets where the title is in the name of the decedent as the *trustee* of a trust;

- assets belonging to the decedent wherein the decedent, by contract, designated a beneficiary or payee in the event of death such as a pension plan, an IRA, a 401(k) plan, or life insurance and the payee survived the decedent; and,

- assets where the title is in the name of the decedent, but have a gross value of $100,000 or less.

Although the above types of properties pass title without probate, they generally do not pass "automatically." See Chapter 2 for an explanation of non-probate properties.

Often a decedent leaves assets that can be transferred at his or her death without probate *and* assets that must be transferred via a probate process.

ESTATE AND INHERITANCE TAXES

There can be federal estate taxes regardless of how a decedent's assets are passed (e.g., under will, living trust, joint tenancy, pensions, life insurance proceeds, etc.) or whether a decedent's assets pass through probate or not through a probate.

A federal estate tax applies in all situations where a decedent's assets have a net value of over $1,000,000. In addition to the $1,000,000 *exemption* amount, assets passing outright (i.e., not in a trust) to a surviving spouse or a qualified charity are generally exempt from the federal estate tax. Certain rules must be followed to qualify property passing to a surviving spouse in a trust or to a surviving spouse who is not a U.S. citizen in order to be exempt from the federal estate tax *beyond* the $1,000,000 exemption amount.

NOTE: *The federal estate tax exemption amount increases from $1,000,000 to $1,500,000 for decedent's dying in 2003, with additional scheduled increases through the year 2009. In 2010, the federal estate tax will be abolished for one year. In 2011, the federal estate tax will return with a $1,000,0000 exemption amount.*

Accordingly, if a decedent has an estate worth $9,000,000 and he or she leaves $6,000,000 to his or her U.S. citizen spouse, $2,000,000 to a qualified charity, and $1,000,000 to his or her best friend, there would be no federal estate tax. The bequests to the spouse and qualified charity would be exempt from taxation and the $1,000,000 to the friend would be equal to the $1,000,000 exemption.

However, if the same decedent instead left $5,000,000 to his or her U.S. citizen spouse, $2,000,000 to a qualified charity, and $2,000,000 to the friend, then the taxable estate, after the $1,000,000 exemption amount, would be $1,000,000. The federal estate tax on the $1,000,000 taxable estate would be about $420,000. The federal estate tax, after the $1,000,000 exemption amount, starts at 39% and increases thereafter.

If the federal estate tax is due, then the federal government assigns a portion of the tax to the state of California. (California used to have a separate inheritance tax, but it was abolished in 1982.)

Do You Need a Lawyer?

You can, of course, hire a lawyer to provide estate tax planning advice and prepare the estate planning documents such as a will. If this is your preference, this book will help you to understand what the lawyer is doing and intelligently communicate your desires.

FINDING A LAWYER

Beware of solicitations from non-lawyers who wish to sell a product, such as an *annuity*, in conjunction with estate planning services. Usually their main goal is the sales commission that goes with the product sale, not the achievement of an appropriate estate plan for you.

It is strongly recommended that you hire a lawyer in the following circumstances:

- The will is likely to be contested; i.e., if you believe that someone may attack the will or any of its provisions after the death of the *testator* (person making the will).

- The estate of the testator exceeds $1,000,000. (Although the forms contained in this book are appropriate for an estate of that size or larger, it makes good sense to consult with an attorney to review other estate planning options which are beyond the scope of this book.)

- If the testator's assets are complicated, such as a *sole proprietorship* or *partnership* business interest. (Again, although the forms contained in this book are appropriate for persons who own business interests, it simply makes sense to discuss those issues with an attorney to review estate planning options which are beyond the scope of this book.)

- The testator wishes to leave property to a *disqualified* person such as a caregiver or other person who has a fiduciary relationship with the testator or to a non-U.S. citizen surviving spouse. (See Chapter 3 for a discussion of disqualified persons.)

- There are questions about the mental capacity of the testator to sign the will.

The California Bar Association certifies specialists in estate planning and can give you a list of the certified specialists in your area. A lawyer becomes a certified specialist by proof of experience in the area of certification and passing a test. It is no secret that lawyers who are knowledgeable in one area of the law may not know much about another area. Therefore, it makes sense to hire a specialist.

As with the choice of anyone you hire, a personal interview, references, costs, and a general feeling of being comfortable with the person should guide you in making the right decision.

ASSETS 2

Not all property that a person owns is actually subject to disposition at their death by a will. This chapter discusses which assets are disposed of at death via a will and which assets are disposed of at death *outside* of the will—regardless of the terms of the will. There is a common misperception that all of a person's assets are disposed of by his or her will. In fact, most property passes title at death without a will, or regardless of the provisions of a will.

ASSETS SUBJECT TO DISPOSITION BY WILL

Assets that can be disposed of by a will include:

- property held in the name of the decedent only without any designation on the title of the asset such as *T.O.D.* (transfer on death), *P.O.D.* (payable on death), *as trustee* (trust).

> ***Warning:*** If the decedent is married and the property in his or her name only is community property, then the decedent can only dispose of the decedent's one-half interest in that property. Simply because one spouse only is listed on the title vesting does not necessarily mean that asset is separate property.

Example: Property with the written title of "Bob" or "Bob, a single man," is typical of property held in the name of the decedent only.

- property held by the decedent and another without any designation on the title or as *tenants in common*.

    Example 1: Property has the written title of "Bob and Mary." In that event, as no type of title is indicated, the law presumes that Bob and Mary are tenants in common, meaning that each owns a separate property interest in the property. As that separate property interest is not identified (i.e., such as 25%), the law presumes they own the property as equal tenants in common—50% each.

    Example 2: Property has the written title of "Bob and Mary, as tenants in common." Bob and Mary are tenants in common, meaning that each owns a separate property interest in the property. As that separate property interest is identified (i.e., as 25%), the law presumes they own the property as equal tenants in common—50% each.

- property held by the decedent and spouse as "husband and wife" or as "community property." This property is community property of the decedent and his or her spouse. In this situation, the decedent can dispose of only his or her one-half community property interest by will.

- one-half of property held in the name of the decedent's spouse if that property is community property.

PROPERTY *SUBJECT* TO DISPOSITION IN A WILL BUT PASSING WITHOUT PROBATE TO A SURVIVING SPOUSE

California is somewhat unique in that it permits all property left outright to a surviving spouse either by will or by intestate succession, to pass without probate. (California Probate Code, beginning with Section 13500.) The estate could be $10,000,000 and if the deceased spouse's will says "all to my spouse" there is no probate in California. However, if there are any restrictions on the use of the property passing to the surviving spouse, i.e., a bequest to a spouse "in trust" or to a "spouse for her lifetime use," then the property is not passing outright to the surviving spouse and the property is subject to probate.

The community property interest of a surviving spouse does not *pass* to the surviving spouse as a result of the death of the predeceasing spouse because the surviving spouse owned it all along, and thus is never probated.

ASSETS *NOT SUBJECT* TO DISPOSITION BY WILL AND PASSING WITHOUT PROBATE

Most property passes title at death without a will (or, regardless of the provisions of a will) and without a probate. Even when there is a probate proceeding, much of the decedent's estate will pass outside of the probate process. The reason the property described in this chapter passes without a will is due to the type of *title vesting* in which the property was held before the death of the decedent.

Example 1: Property has the written title of "Bob and Mary, as joint tenants." That property title is vested in Bob and Mary as joint tenants.

Example 2: Property has the written title of "Bob." That property is title vested in Bob, as an individual (the default for a single person when no other title vesting is given).

JOINT TENANCY   *Joint tenancy* may be the most common way that title to property passes at death without the need of a will and without the need of probate. In California, property can be held in the names of two or more persons as joint tenants.

To be joint tenancy property, it must be written in the title—i.e., no verbal joint tenancies. (California Civil Code Section 683.) Sometimes the initials "JTWROS," *joint tenants with right of survivorship*, is used to designate joint tenancy property. There is a limited exception to the rule that the words joint tenancy must appear on the title: car/boat titles using the word "or" or "and/or" means, by statute, "joint tenancy."

Example: Property with a written title "Bob and Mary, as joint tenants" or "Bob and Mary, husband and wife, JTWROS" is joint tenancy property. Property with a written title "Bob and Mary as husband and wife" or "Bob and Mary as tenants in common" is not joint tenancy property.

Title to joint tenancy property at the death of one of the joint tenants passes to the surviving joint tenant(s). Accordingly, all the surviving joint tenant(s) has to do to acquire the decedent joint tenant's interest is to survive the deceased joint tenant.

> *Warning:* Community property held in joint tenancy between a deceased spouse and someone other than the surviving spouse is, at the death of the deceased spouse, subject to the community property interest claim to one-half of the property by the surviving spouse because the deceased spouse did not have the right to dispose of the surviving spouse's community property interest in the joint tenancy property. *In this event contact a lawyer.*

NOTE: *Property held in joint tenancy is equally owned by each joint tenant. If a parent deeds his residence to himself and his child as joint tenants, the child becomes a one-half owner of the property. Even if the parent is still living, the creditors of that child could* attach *the residence or the child could demand the residence be sold and the proceeds equally divided. In addition, most transfers into joint tenancy are considered "gifts" for federal gift tax purposes except when the asset is a bank account or the joint tenants are spouses.*

P.O.D. BANK ACCOUNTS AND T.O.D. BROKERAGE ACCOUNTS

Payable on death bank accounts and transfer on death brokerage accounts also transfer without a will (and regardless of the provisions of the will) at the death of the owner of the account. Of course, the account must be held in the name of the owner with the designation "payable on death" or "transfer on death." The difference between joint tenancy and a P.O.D. or T.O.D. account is that the beneficiary of the P.O.D. or T.O.D. account has no rights to the property until the death of the owner. Whereas, a joint tenant is, legally, an equal co-owner of the property before the death of the other joint tenant. (California Probate Code 5100 through 5512).

> ***Warning:*** If someone other than the surviving spouse is the named beneficiary of a P.O.D. or T.O.D. account in the name of a deceased spouse, the surviving spouse has a claim for his or her community property interest in the account, if the account was community property of the deceased spouse and the surviving spouse. *In this event, contact a lawyer.*

LIFE INSURANCE, ANNUITIES, PENSIONS, IRAS, PRIVATE RETIREMENT ACCOUNTS

Life insurance, annuities, pensions, individual retirement accounts (IRAs), and private retirement accounts are all examples of property which passes at death based upon a contract and not pursuant to the provisions in a will. The owner of the contract, i.e., the insured or the annuitant, in essence contracts with the insurer, employer, or plan administrator to pay the proceeds to a beneficiary that was designated as the recipient in the event of his or her death.

In the event that a beneficiary has not been designated, some contracts will designate a "default" beneficiary such as the spouse, children, etc. At the death of the person insured, the beneficiary need only execute the appropriate claim forms and submit a certified copy of the decedent's death certificate to claim the benefits that will not need to go through probate.

> ***Warning:*** If someone other than the surviving spouse is the named beneficiary and any portion of the contractual proceeds are community property or the premiums that paid for the contract were community property, then the surviving spouse has a claim for his or her community property interest in the proceeds or contract. *In this event, contact a lawyer.*

TOTTEN TRUST
ACCOUNTS

A bank account can be held in the name of the account owner "as trustee for" or "in trust for" a named beneficiary. In this situation, the "trustee" (i.e., the owner of the account) has created a "mini" revocable trust for the account commonly called a *totten trust*. In the event of the death of the account owner, the named beneficiary becomes the owner of the account without the need of a probate. If the account is held in the name of two persons as joint tenants "as trustees for" or "in trust for" a named beneficiary and one of the account owners dies, the surviving account owner, as the surviving joint tenant, owns all of the account and can revoke the account and/or change the named beneficiary.

> *Warning:* If someone other than the surviving spouse of the account holder is the named beneficiary and where the totten trust account contains community property, the surviving spouse of the account holder has a claim for his or her community property interest in the account. *In this event, contact a lawyer.*

LIVING TRUST

Property titled in the name of a *living trust* or property declared to be in a living trust when the *trustor* (the person that created and transferred the property to the trust) and the *trustee* (the one who administers and manages the trust property) is the same person is not subject to probate. The title to property in a living trust might read something like: "John Smith, Trustee of the Smith Family Trust dated 4/2/01."

One of the main purposes of creating a living trust is to avoid probate. Upon the death of the trustor, the trustee (often a successor trustee as the trustor is usually the trustee until he or she dies) administers and distributes the living trust estate pursuant to the written instructions in the living trust document. The will of the trustor cannot dispose of the property held by the trust, as title to the property in the trust is held by the trust.

If the trustor declares in the living trust that certain property is part of the living trust, but fails to actually change the title of the property to the name of the living trust, a simple action can be brought in the probate court to have such property declared to be part of the living trust. In this event a lawyer should be consulted.

Small Estate Distribution

If we exclude all of the decedent's property passing outright to a surviving spouse, passing under joint tenancy survivorship, P.O.D or T.O.D.
account designations, totten trusts, a living trust, and by contract (life
insurance, pensions, retirement plans, IRAs and annuities), then what is
left should go through probate. However, if the gross value of those
properties (real property and personal property combined) that should
go through probate is *under $100,000*, then they also may pass to the
beneficiary or heir without probate. On the other hand, if the gross
value of those properties which should go through probate is *over*
$100,000, then all of the property that should go through probate
must go through probate (California Probate Code, beginning with
Sec. 13100.).

Coordinating Your Estate Plan— Your Will and Your Non-Will Assets

Before preparing your will, it is a good idea to use the Asset Roadmap
(Appendix B) to list your assets and the manner that you hold title to
the assets. Remembering that assets held in joint tenancy, T.O.D.,
P.O.D., totten trusts, living trusts, pension plans, IRAs, 401(k)s (and
other retirement plans), insurance, and annuities can pass to your
intended beneficiary at death without a will might result in your decision to change the title vesting to allow certain assets you own to transfer at death without probate.

Example: Rather than holding a brokerage account in the name of
"Bob," have the brokerage firm change the title to "Bob, transfer on death to Mary." Then, Mary would receive the assets
without probate and regardless of any contrary provisions in
Bob's will.

> **Warning:** Creating a joint tenancy title is not recommended for property that is owned in your name only. If this occurs, the other joint tenant becomes a one-half owner of the property during your lifetime and subject to possible federal gift tax issues.

Even if you effectively title all of your assets to permit their passing at your death to beneficiaries without the need of a will, you should still consider preparing and executing a will as a "back-up." This can beneficial for assets you may later acquire and fail to title in a manner that permits the asset to pass at your death without the need of a will.

When preparing the will, consider the total inheritance of each beneficiary based upon what that beneficiary receives under the will and what that beneficiary receives outside of the will, e.g., as an insurance beneficiary.

Example: Bob's will gives Mary 25% of the $500,000 in assets subject to Bob's will. Bob's $300,000 life insurance policy names Mary as the sole beneficiary. Bob dies. Mary receives $425,000 ($125,000 under Bob's will and $300,000 from Bob's life insurance) from Bob's $800,000 estate (over 53% of Bob's estate), which is much more than the 25% she receives under Bob's will.

BENEFICIARIES 3

This chapter discusses who or what *can* inherit from your will and who or what *cannot* inherit from your will. For example, you cannot leave money to your dog, Fido, but you could leave money to a friend for the purpose of taking care of Fido. This chapter will also discuss the problems in leaving property to persons who are under the age of 18, persons who are considered *disqualified* to inherit and what you can do to make them qualified to inherit, and your rights to disinherit persons.

WHO AND WHAT CAN INHERIT

PERSONS   You can leave your property to any person, regardless of their age, where they live, or their status.

Example 1: You can leave your property to a cousin in North Korea. However, North Korea may not allow the beneficiary to receive the bequest or may take the bequest from the beneficiary.

Example 2: You can leave property to a friend in state prison.

There are certain persons who are considered to be disqualified persons unless you take certain steps to qualify the bequest to them, as discussed on page 21.

You do *not* have to leave your one-half interest in community property or any of your separate property to your spouse or your children. On the other hand, you *cannot* leave your spouse's one-half interest in community property to someone else, as your spouse owns that property.

GOVERNMENT

You can leave your property to any governmental entity in the United States.

Example: A bequest to the city of Costa Mesa is legal.

NON-PROFIT ORGANIZATIONS

You can leave your property to a non-profit organization such as a charity.

Example: A bequest to the American Red Cross or the SPCA is legal.

WHO AND WHAT CANNOT INHERIT

You can't take it with you, but you cannot leave your property to certain types of organizations and animals.

PARTNERSHIP

You cannot leave your property to a partnership. However, you can leave your property to the *individuals* of a partnership.

CORPORATION

You cannot leave your property to a corporation.

ANIMALS

You cannot leave your property to an animal. However, you can leave your property to a person or non-profit organization in trust to care for an animal.

SPECIAL LIMITATIONS ON BEQUESTS TO MINORS

If you leave your property to a minor, the court appoints a *guardian* of the minor's estate to manage the bequest (and any other assets of the minor) until the minor attains 18 years of age. At that time the property is delivered, outright, to the former minor. Guardianships are "safe" in that the court appointed guardian must post a *surety bond* to insure the minor's estate against any dishonesty of the guardian. The guardian must file an account to the court of the minor's assets every two years.

On the other hand, it costs money to create the guardianship through the court, to obtain a surety bond, and to file the required accountings to the court. However, the biggest problem to guardianships is that they end when the minor attains 18 years of age. Most eighteen-year-olds are too young to manage their assets. Fortunately, there are several alternatives to court supervised guardianships of a minor's estate.

UNIFORM TRANSFER TO MINOR'S ACT

Under the *Uniform Transfer to Minor's Act* (Probate Code, beginning with Section 3900), sometimes called the *Uniform Gift to Minor's Act*, you can bequeath property to an adult person as *custodian* to hold for the benefit of the minor. This is an *informal trust arrangement*. The custodian, who is not under automatic court supervision, is required by law to hold and manage the property for the minor's benefit only. The custodian delivers the property to the minor at an age directed by you—up to age 25.

Example: "I bequeath $10,000 to Bob Smith, as custodian under the Uniform Transfer to Minor's Act for the benefit of Terry Smith until Terry Smith attains 25 years of age."

Forms are provided for bequests to a custodian for a minor's benefit in Appendix D. Leaving property to a custodian avoids the court costs and court supervision involved in guardianships. Also, the custodians can hold the property for the minor past his or her 18th birthday, if you direct. However, if you fail to specify an age for distribution, the custodian *must* distribute the property to the former minor when he or she turns 18 years old.

The disadvantage of custodianships is the lack of mandatory court filed accountings and bonds. Accordingly, you must be very careful in the selection of the custodian. You should consider requiring that the custodian post a surety bond as a condition of his or her appointment.

IRC 529
COLLEGE PLANS

Congress recently enacted legislation that permits states to create and administer college education investment plans. Most states, like California, offer different investment options within their plan. Most investment plans are essentially mutual stock and/or bond funds. In California there is no sales commission involved (i.e., "load" cost) to buy (if you purchase directly through the state program) or to withdraw. The annual management fee is under 1%. Some of the benefits of these plans are:

- the assets in the plans earn income tax deferred (federal and state) until the monies are withdrawn, and

- the income earned is not taxed (federal) upon withdrawal if the withdrawn funds are used for a "qualified higher educational expense" in college. A "qualified higher educational expense" includes books, tuition, school room/board, and even many off-campus living expenses.

In an *IRC 529 college plan*, the plan contributor names someone to manage the plan, i.e., to determine when and what expenses to pay. That person is called the *plan participant*. The beneficiary of the plan is called the *plan beneficiary*. Forms in Appendix D permit a custodian or a trustee for a beneficiary to distribute property they manage into a 529 college plan.

NOTE: *The IRC 529 college plans can be created by contributions during lifetime as well. To learn more, go to California's website for its IRC 529 college plan at **www.scholarshare.org**.*

TRUST

You can leave property to a trustee to hold in trust for the benefit of the minor until the minor reaches a more mature age for distribution. In many ways, a trust is like custodianship. A trust avoids automatic court involvement and supervision like custodianship. However, unlike a custodianship, a trust can be created for a beneficiary who is not a minor, can delay final distribution beyond age 25, and permits you to place greater conditions and restrictions on the use of the property.

For example, you can direct the trustee to pay educational expenses of the beneficiary and/or permit the trustee to withhold a distribution if the beneficiary fails a reasonable drug and/or alcohol abuse test. See the forms in Appendix D for trusts for minors.

DISQUALIFIED BENEFICIARIES

California, by statute, disqualifies bequests to certain individuals based upon their involvement in the making of the will, relationship to the person making the will, or their occupation. Probate Code Section 21350 disqualifies bequests to:

- the person who drafted the will (and the employees, law partners, cohabitants, and certain relatives of said person);

- any person who has a "fiduciary" relationship with the testator, who transcribes the will or causes the will to be transcribed (and employees, cohabitants, and certain relatives of said persons); and,

- any "care custodian" of a "dependent adult."

The disqualified bequest becomes *qualified* if:

- the disqualified person is related by blood to you within five degrees. (Your parent is related to you within one degree. Your sibling is related to you within two degrees, your nephew is related to you within three degrees, etc.);

- the disqualified person cohabitates with you (as husband, wife, or gay partner);

- you receive a written *certificate of independent review* of the document from a lawyer after the lawyer reviews the otherwise disqualified transfer with you; or,

- the disqualified person can prove in court by clear and convincing evidence that the bequest was not the product of undue influence, fraud, or duress.

Generally, a disqualified person is involved in the preparation of the will in question or is related to the person involved in the preparation of the will. However, the "care custodian" of a "dependent adult" category is a trap for the unwary. The term "care custodian" essentially means anyone who has ever helped an adult. The term "dependent adult" means any person whose mental or physical capacities have diminished at all during their lifetime. The care custodian does not have to be involved in the preparation of the will in which he or she is left a bequest. Nor does the care custodian have to ever give assistance to the testator. In sum, every adult person is a "care custodian" of a "dependent adult." Accordingly, by statute in California, every beneficiary of a will is arguably a disqualified person as a care custodian of a dependent adult unless one of the qualifying exceptions above is met.

Example: "I leave $1,000.00 to my gardener, Bob Smith." This bequest violates the statute and is disqualified unless the gardener cohabitates with you (as husband, wife, or gay partner), is related to you within five degrees, or you receive a written certificate of independent review as to said bequest from a lawyer.

Warning: An attorney's written Certificate of Independent Review is essential if you want to leave a bequest to a potentially "disqualified" person.

Warning: Probate Code Section 21350 is not limited to bequests under a will. It also applies to lifetime gift transfers and transfers by trusts, joint tenancies, life insurance, etc.

After Born Children and Subsequent Spouses

California Probate Code Sections 21610–21623 provide that in many situations a spouse or child acquired after the date of the execution of a will are considered to be "forgotten" by the testator and, therefore, entitled to their intestate succession share of the testator's estate.

Example: Bob, a single man with one child, executes a will leaving everything to his one child. Bob then married Sue. Bob dies on his honeymoon with Sue. Bob fails to amend or execute a new will after he marries Sue. Under California law, Sue is now entitled to that share of Bob's estate (i.e., 50% in this case) that she would have received if Bob had no will regardless of the fact that Bob's will leaves everything to his one child.

Who You Can Disinherit

You do not have to leave your estate to someone you do not want to even if that person is your spouse or your child. You have the right to *disinherit* anybody.

Disinheritance Clause

Paragraph THIRD of the will forms in this book uses a comprehensive disinheritance clause which disinherits all persons other than those specifically named as beneficiaries in the will. Accordingly, if someone shows up after your death claiming to be your long lost brother, he is still subject to the disinheritance clause and would receive no part of your estate.

WHO CAN CONTEST YOUR WILL

Although you have the right to disinherit anyone, certain persons can contest your will claiming:

- that the will was improperly executed;

- that you lacked mental competency to execute a will;

- that the will was the result of fraud; or,

- that you were unduly influenced.

Only certain persons have the right to contest your will. The persons who can contest your will are:

- those persons who would take your estate if there were no will (i.e., your heirs) and,

- those persons who received a bequest from you under a prior will.

Example: You are single with one adult child. Your child has two children. Your first and only will leaves everything to your brother. Your child, the person who would take you property if there were no will, has the legal right to contest your will. Your grandchildren do not have the right to contest your will as they would not inherit your property if your will was declared to be invalid.

ANTI-CONTEST CLAUSE

Each of the will forms in this book have a second part to paragraph THIRD, the *Anti-Contest clause*, which disinherits not only anyone who "contests" the will, but also disinherits anyone who "contests" non-will transfers such as joint tenancies, T.O.D. securities accounts, or life insurance. It even disinherits persons who make claims against your estate for services rendered or agreements to share property.

Therefore, the only persons truly affected by the anti-contest clause are the persons who have something to lose under your will if they contest it and lose, i.e., the beneficiaries. A beneficiary who receives 10% of your estate under your will but who would be entitled to 25% of your estate if you died without a will is affected by the anti-contest clause and thus must make a decision whether to *not* contest the will and take the 10% or to contest the will and possibly lose the 10%.

The anti-contest clause is only effective against persons who are beneficiaries under your will as everyone else has already been disinherited under your disinheritance clause. The anti-contest clause does not prohibit anyone from contesting the will; it simply states that anybody who "contests" your will is disinherited. If a person is *not* a beneficiary of your estate, they have nothing to lose under the anti-contest clause.

BEQUEST INCENTIVES YOUR WILL TO AVOID CONTESTS

Will contests are messy and expensive legal matters. Yet, as discussed above, the anti-contest clause only helps to prevent will contests by persons who have something to lose. Accordingly, if you want to disinherit an heir (i.e., a person who would take a portion or all of your estate if there was no will), consider leaving that heir a small bequest as a *incentive* not to contest the will.

Example: You dislike your son, one of the two heirs to you estate, and want to leave all of your property to your other heir. However, you know that the disinherited son, being the jerk that he is, will contest your will simply to exact an emotional and financial toll on the beneficiary of your property. You could decide to leave the son you dislike $10,000 in your will with the anti-contest clause. At your death, the son you dislike now has a dilemma. If he contests the will and loses the contest he also loses the $10,000 bequest.

Obviously, the amount of the incentive will differ depending on the value of your estate and the potential anger of the person you dislike.

BEQUESTS 4

Each time you dispose of property in your will, you are said to be making a *bequest*. The act of making a bequest is "to bequeath." Historically, a bequest was a gift in will of personal property and a *devise* was a gift in a will of real estate. Later, the California Probate Code decided that all gifts in a will were devises. However, because of the common usage of the word "bequest," that term is used exclusively in this book.

This chapter discusses three separate, and often intermingled topics, about bequests. First we will discuss the difference between a *specific bequest* and a *residual bequest*. As part of that topic, we will discuss the difference between *tangible personal property*, *intangible personal property*, and *real property*.

Finally, this chapter will discuss various ways property can be left to beneficiaries:

- outright (no strings attached);

- with conditions;

- in a "life estate;" or,

- in trust (including custodianships).

SPECIFIC AND RESIDUAL BEQUESTS

Regardless of other categorizations, bequests are either *specific* or *residual*.

SPECIFIC
BEQUESTS

Specific bequests are where the property bequeathed is specifically identified by item (i.e., my 1974 Ford Pinto), by type (i.e., all of my household furnishings), or by amount (i.e., $100,000). Specific bequests can be further described by the type of property.

TANGIBLE
PERSONAL
PROPERTY

Personal property you can touch, move, or hold such a cars, clothes, household items are called *tangible, personal property*. I discourage bequeathing specifically identified items of personal, tangible property such as "my pink couch in my living room" for several reasons.

- First, said items may be sold, discarded, or gifted before your death, which then raises the question whether the beneficiary is to get the new "green couch" in your living room.

- Second, if the specifically identified property cannot be found after your death, your executor must either explain to the court if he or she knows what happened to the property, or make diligent efforts to locate the specifically identified property and describe those efforts to the court.

- Finally, if you do own the specifically identified property at the time of your death, your executor will have to have it separately appraised and separately inventoried on any federal estate tax returns filed with the IRS and any probate inventories filed with the probate court, which may result in an increased value (bad for tax purposes) as well as an additional cost of appraisal. Sometimes the cost of appraisal can exceed the value of the item.

On the other hand, a beneficiary of your highly valued Van Gogh painting may want it to be specifically devised, appraised, and inventoried for income tax basis purposes, insurance purposes, and to later be able to prove how he acquired title to the painting.

In paragraph SECOND of the will forms, you have the opportunity to make a specific bequest of tangible, personal property. Therefore, you *can* bequeath your Van Gogh painting or "green couch in your living room" if you wish.

After the listing of any specific bequests of tangible, personal property, paragraph SECOND permits you to bequeath the remaining (or all, if you made no specific bequests) of the tangible, personal property to one or more persons or entities, in equal shares.

Occasionally, the division of the personal, tangible property among the family members can be the most troublesome part of the distribution of a your estate. Although the dollar amount may be small, sentimental attachment or long-term resentments are often involved. In those situations, you may wish to prepare an informal note advising the beneficiaries of how you want certain items of tangible, personal property to be distributed and keep that note with your will. Although the note may not be legally enforceable, it could guide reasonable beneficiaries.

INTANGIBLE PERSONAL PROPERTY

Intangible personal property includes cash, securities accounts, securities, partnership interests, promissory notes, and business interests that are merely representative of value. Paragraph SECOND in the will forms permits the bequeathing of intangible personal property.

I discourage bequests of specific, non-cash, intangible personal property such as "my 500 shares of IBM stock" as the stock could, before your death, be sold, had a 3 for 1 stock split, or changed substantially in value. Remember the maxim, "A will speaks as of date of death."

On the other hand, cash bequests, assuming the cash will be available at your death, are not a problem.

Example: "I bequeath ten thousand dollars ($10,000.00) to Bob Smith."

REAL PROPERTY

Improved and unimproved real estate, including mineral interests and condo stock co-ops, are all *real property*. I discourage the bequeathing of specific parcels of real property as it may be sold or exchanged before your death or its value or mortgage encumbrances may materially change from time to time.

However, Paragraph SECOND permits bequeathing specific real property. If such a bequest is made, you must decide whether the real property is to be distributed to the beneficiary subject to all mortgages on the real property or whether your estate is to pay-off the mortgages for the beneficiary.

RESIDUAL
BEQUESTS

Residual bequests dispose of the *residue* of your estate. The residue is *what is left* in the estate after payment of all costs of the administration of your estate, all of your debts, and all of your specific bequests in your will. In many wills, the residue is the largest portion of the estate and sometimes, in those cases where there are no specific bequests, the residue is the *entire* estate. Because the residue includes *what is left*, it includes both real property and all types of personal property.

If there is more than one residual beneficiary, you need to determine what portion of the residue each beneficiary is to receive. The interest of each beneficiary need not be the same as another.

Example: You could leave Bob 10% of the residue and Mary 90% of the residue.

Instead of listing the interest of each beneficiary in terms of a percentage of the residue, I recommend using *shares*. The reason I use shares is because one or more of the residual beneficiaries might die before you. If each share represents a fraction of the residue, then regardless of whether any shares lapse, it is easy to determine what each beneficiary receives. You might find this concept easier to conceptualize if you start with 100 shares, as each share then equals 1%. If a bequest of 5 shares, for example, lapses due to the death of the beneficiary before you, then there are 95 shares and each share is worth 1/95, slightly more than 1%.

Example: "I devise all of the rest of my estate as follows:
    A. 25 shares to Bob Smith;
    B. 10 shares to Mary Jones;
    C. 65 shares to John Doe.
If any of the above persons die before my death their devise shall lapse."

In the example, if all three beneficiaries survive you, Bob will get 25% of the residue, Mary will get 10% of the residue, and John will get 65% of the residue. If Bob and Mary survive the decedent, but John does not, then Bob will get 25/35 of the residue (about 78%) and Mary will get 10/35 (about 22%).

CONDITIONAL OUTRIGHT BEQUESTS

So far, we have been discussing unconditional outright bequests. However, outright bequests can have conditions attached. Generally, conditions are *conditions precedent*, that is, a condition that must be met before delivery of the bequest. For example, a condition that a bequest not be paid until the beneficiary graduates from a university is valid, but may substantially delay the delivery of the bequest.

Conditions cannot be illegal or against public policy. For example, a condition that the beneficiary do an illegal act—such as murder some-one—would be illegal and non-enforceable. A condition that the beneficiary not marry anyone of Hungarian heritage would also be a violation of anti-discrimination laws and thus unenforceable. However, a condition that a beneficiary not marry a specific individual *is* enforceable. I recommend *against* imposing any conditions to bequests, however, if you wish to do so, you should seek the expertise of a lawyer.

The most common condition to a bequest is that of surviving the testa-tor by a certain period of time. Where applicable, the will forms in this book have used a 30-day survivorship requirement.

What happens if the survivorship requirement is not met? By law, if nothing is said, the bequest to a beneficiary who fails to meet the sur-vivorship requirement either lapses (the bequest is not made if the beneficiary is not a blood relative of the decedent or the decedent's spouse of the decedent's former spouse) or is paid to the issue of the deceased beneficiary. This occurs if that beneficiary is a blood relative of the decedent or the decedent's spouse of the decedent's former spouse to the decedent by the second degree (i.e., parent, grandparent, sibling, child, grandchild). (California Probate Code, Sec. 21110.) Spouses of deceased beneficiaries are not "issue" and receive nothing unless specified to receive the bequest by the testator in the event the primary beneficiary fails the survivorship requirement.

NOTE: *Sometimes older wills condition a bequest on the beneficiary "surviving distribution." This results in a "chicken and egg" argument. If the beneficiary is not living at the actual time of distribution, the court cannot order the distribution.*

LIFE ESTATE

Sometimes you want the beneficiary to have only the right to use the property for his or her lifetime, and then have the property distributed to a second beneficiary after the death of the first beneficiary. The beneficiary using the property for his or her lifetime is called the *life tenant.* The beneficiary who takes the property after the death of the life tenant is called the *remainderman.*

Although any type of property can be subject to a life estate, the most common situation involves the use of residential real property.

Example: You bequeath your daughter a life estate in your residence. Your daughter has the right to use your residence after your death, for the remainder of her lifetime. Your daughter could live in the residence, rent the residence to others (however, she could not rent the residence for a period of time beyond her lifetime), or even sell her life estate (the buyer of a life estate buys only the right to use the property during the lifetime of the selling life tenant).

During her life estate your daughter, as the life tenant, would pay all interest (but not principal) on any encumbrance on the property, association dues, normal repairs, insurance, and property taxes.

After the death of the life tenant, the remainderman becomes the absolute owner of the property. Sometimes, in a second marriage situation, a spouse leaves the surviving spouse a life estate in the predeceasing spouse's residence with the remaindermen being the children of the predeceasing spouse's prior marriage.

IN TRUST

A *trust* is an often-misunderstood term. There are many types of trusts. The *living trust* is used as a will substitute to avoid probate. The *martial deduction trust* is used to minimize and defer federal estate taxes. But the trusts utilized in the will forms contained in this book are used by married couples on the death of the first spouse to die in order to manage assets for the benefit of one beneficiary until he or she either receives the trust assets upon attaining a designated age or he or she dies and the trust estate is delivered to a second beneficiary.

In many ways, the trusts used in the will forms contained in this book work like the life estate discussed above, with some exceptions.

- First, a trust is a more convenient method of handling a group of assets, especially a residual interest in an estate, rather than multiple life estates, one for each property.

- Second, a trust places the legal title to property in the hands of a trustee to manage for the beneficiary rather than relying on the beneficiary to properly manage the property. (In many cases, the beneficiary is too financially unsophisticated to manage the property.)

- Third, the trust provides flexibility in distributions during the life of the trust (e.g., more than simply "income" can be distributed to the beneficiary) and can provide for distributions to the beneficiary upon the beneficiary attaining a specified age.

The will forms in Appendix D provide for trusts of residual shares of the estate for a spouse, child, or friend. Some of the will forms provide for the beneficiary to receive discretionary payment of principal for illnesses as well as the "income" of the trust. If you want greater flexibility as to distributions from the trust to the beneficiaries, you need to consult with a lawyer to draft your will. Of course, as with any bequest in your will, the funding and administration of the trust created by your will does not occur until after your death.

5

Selecting the People Who Will Carry Out Your Wishes

A *fiduciary* is someone who owes a duty of loyalty and fairness to another. It is a position of trust wherein the fiduciary cannot take a financial or personal advantage. This chapter discusses three types of fiduciaries: the guardian, the executor, and the trustee or custodian.

Guardian

You have the right to nominate a *guardian* to care for your minor children after your death. There are two types of guardians. First, there is the guardian of the "person." The guardian of the person is responsible for the minor's housing, food, clothing, etc. Then there is the guardian of the "estate." The guardian of the minor's estate manages any assets of the minor.

Only persons can be appointed by the court to be a guardian of a minor's person. However, corporate trustees (i.e. trust companies) as well as persons can be appointed by the court to be a guardian of a minor's estate. The guardian of the person and the guardian of the estate do not have to be the same person. Guardianships of person and estate both end when the minor reaches the age of 18.

You have the right to nominate a guardian of a minor's person only if there is no natural parent of the minor living (unless the natural parent is legally determined to be unfit). Some divorced, custodial parents incorrectly believe they have the right to nominate a guardian for the person of their minor children in the event of their own death.

Minors, aged 14 years and older, have the right to express a preference for the guardian of their person. You, the parent of the minor, have only the right to *nominate* a guardian. Only the superior court can appoint a guardian. The court will consider your written nomination of a guardian, but the appointment of the guardian will be based upon what the court determines to be "in the best interest of the minor." In short, your nomination of a guardian is not legally binding on the court.

SELECTION OF THE GUARDIAN OF THE PERSON

Obviously, it is wise to verify with a prospective guardian that he or she is willing to act. In addition, you must be comfortable with the lifestyle choices of the prospective guardian. Sometimes best friends would make the worst guardians. In selecting a guardian of the person for a minor child consider the following questions.

- Does the guardian live near the minor's family members? It might be wiser to select your cousin who lives near the minor's family members than a sister who lives on the other side of the nation.

- Is there religious compatibility between the guardian and your child?

- If the child is older, is the proximity of the guardian's residence to the friends and school of the child important?

- What is the age of the prospective guardians? Your mother may be too old to handle your minor child.

- What is the family situation of the guardian? Your friends with the 2-year-old quintuplets might be too busy with their children to act as guardians for your 13-year-old twins.

- Is the issue of divorce a consideration on your selection? If you choose Mary Smith who is married at the time of the nomination, do you still want her to act if, at the time of your death, she is divorced or married to someone new?

- Is there a problem of nominating a husband and wife as co-guardians? Which one might or should continue as guardian if they divorce after your death? Consider nominating only the husband or the wife as guardian to avoid confusion over your intent in the event that person and his or her spouse later divorce.

INSTRUCTIONS TO THE NOMINATED GUARDIAN

As the court acts in the "best interest of the child," the nominated guardian should be aware beforehand of their nomination and should have at least a copy of your NOMINATION OF GUARDIAN for their use if necessary. (see form 1, p.107.) You need to tell the proposed guardian that, in the event of your death, no one is automatically going to hand them your children, nor is the court going to appoint them without the proposed guardian petitioning the court to do so. In the event of your death, the nominated guardian needs to immediately take physical possession of the minor and petition the court for temporary guardianship of each minor's person pending the court hearing on the appointment of the permanent guardian.

Persons you might *not* want to act as guardians for your children, often become the guardians simply because they acted more quickly than your nominated guardian. Many judges refuse to move a minor child from the custody of the first person to take possession of the child after the death of the child's parent to avoid a further disruption of the minor child's life.

USE OF THE NOMINATION OF GUARDIAN FORMS

As there is no requirement that your nomination of a guardian for a minor's person be in a will, the two NOMINATION OF GUARDIAN forms in this book are designed to be used to independently of the will. One of the reasons I prefer the separate NOMINATION OF GUARDIAN form is that at least a copy of the form should be given to the nominated guardian. By using a separate form, the nominated guardian does not have a copy of your will.

The first form is your basic guardianship nomination form when you do not expect any conflict over the nomination. The second form contains additional language and should be used when you suspect there may be a conflict over the appointment of the guardian, and the appointment of a particular guardian is of the utmost importance to you. Both forms provide that the same person is nominated to act as guardian of your minor child's person and estate.

If you want to nominate different guardians, one for the estate of a minor and a different one for the person of a minor, simply use the guardianship forms found in this book twice and cross through and initial the word "person" or "estate" as appropriate to create two guardianship nominations forms, one for the person of your minor children and one for the estate of your minor children.

EXECUTORS

An *executor* is the person or *corporate fiduciary* (i.e., trust company) that is appointed under your will to manage your estate after you die. The executor will offer your will to the court for probate; marshal your assets; file an inventory of your assets with the court; and, pay all debts, expenses of administration, and taxes. The executor will also sell any property necessary to put the estate in a position to be closed, at which time the executor will petition the court to make an order to distribute your estate. During the probate of your estate, the executor has the duties to account for the financial transactions of the estate and to keep the court and the beneficiaries informed as to the progress of the estate administration.

After the court issues the order for distribution, the executor will distribute your estate pursuant to the terms of that order which incorporates the asset disposition provisions of your will. The term executor is used when that person or trust company was appointed under a will. If the person or trust company is not named under a will, then that person or trust company is called an *administrator*. (Years ago the above terms referred only to men or trust companies. Women were referred to as an executrix or an administratrix. In recent years there has been a tendency to refer to executors, executrixes, administrators and administratrixes all simply as "personal representatives.")

A will does not have to nominate an executor to be valid. However, nomination in your will of the executor permits you to select the executor and permits you to determine whether the executor should or should not be bonded.

SELECTING YOUR EXECUTOR

Carefully select your executor. Too many people feel that the job is merely honorary and that competence is a secondary consideration. Nothing could be further from the truth. A good executor will make the difference between an estate that is handled efficiently and expeditiously versus an estate that will bog down into eventual litigation and losses. A good executor is one who keeps detailed financial records, is not a procrastinator, and can make difficult decisions. Although the executor will most likely hire a lawyer to assist him, the responsibility begins with and ends with the executor.

If you do not have someone you trust and who fits the above description to select as your executor, consider naming a trust company to act as the executor. Most banks have trust companies as part of their operations. The primary objections to trust companies are that they are impersonal and they charge the statutory fee. Being impersonal can be a good thing as executors that are afraid to hurt feelings, etc., can end up as the worst executors. As to the fee, family or friends who act as executor may also take the statutory fee and they should, being an executor is work and the fee is earned.

The "statutory fee" is the fee permitted by the court for the ordinary work done by the executor in an estate. The fee is 4% on the first $100,000 of gross value of the estate, 3% on the next $100,000, 2% on the next $800,000, 1% on the next $1,000,000, etc.

Trust companies are professionals. They have created systems to keep track of all transactions and progress of the estate. Unlike some persons, corporate fiduciaries do not wait until the end of the month to make income deposits, they keep records of financial transactions, and they do not steal the estate assets. However, if your estate is under $200,000 most trust companies will decline to act, as the statutory fee is too small.

SURETY BONDS

Many lawyers will tell you that if you cannot trust a person enough to waive the requirement of posting a *surety bond* as the executor, then you should not appoint that person as the executor. I disagree. Bonds often help keep an executor honest and no honest executor would object to posting a surety bond.

The surety bond posted by the executor is in an amount equal to the value of the personal property of estate (real property does not have to be bonded as it cannot be sold without consent of the beneficiaries or the court), and is an inexpensive form of insurance to guarantee that the executor will act honestly. The cost of such a bond is relatively modest, i.e., $1200 per year for a $200,000 bond, but adds financial protection to the estate and the benefit of the concern of the bonding company.

The bonding company does not want to lose money. Accordingly, the bonding company checks the credit history of the executor. If the credit report of the executor is not "A+," the bonding company may sometimes require the executor to give the bonding company joint control over major estate assets to lessen the bonding company liability exposure. Bonds are especially important when you have minors as beneficiaries of the estate, as they usually are unable to ascertain if the estate is being mishandled or not and are the ones most adversely affected by a dishonest executor.

WAIVER OF
PUBLICATION OF
INTENT TO SELL

In the will forms in this book, paragraph FOURTH is the nomination of executor paragraph. In that paragraph you waive the requirement of publishing a legal notice in a newspaper each time the executor wishes to sell estate property. This publication is a formality that costs money and time, but does not protect the estate or assist in obtaining the highest price for the property sold. The waiving of the publication requirement *does not* give the executor the right to sell property without either the permission of all affected beneficiaries under the will or the court.

TRUSTEES AND CUSTODIANS

As described above, the executor manages your estate after death during the probate process. The trustee receives, from the executor of your will, property at the end of the probate of your estate and then manages that property for the benefit of the trust's beneficiaries that you named in your will. The trustee has legal title to the property under his or her control and can buy or sell assets without permission from the court or the beneficiaries. Unlike an executor, the trustee is not automatically under the jurisdiction of the court. Like an executor, the trustee must render accountings to the beneficiaries and must keep the beneficiaries informed. The trustee is entitled to reasonable compensation for his or her services, but may make no other profit at the expense of the trust.

Example: A trustee who is a realtor cannot claim a sales commission for selling trust real estate.

Unlike the short tenure of an executor (it usually takes one year to probate an estate), a trustee might act for a substantial number of years. In addition, unlike an executor, a trustee generally does not rely upon an attorney for the day-to-day management of the trust.

I have even greater concerns about the appointment of your trustee, as they hold the assets for a greater period of time and the court does not supervise them. I strongly suggest you consider requiring your trustee to post a surety bond, an option you have in the will forms in Appendix D.

Custodians are nearly the same as trustees except that custodians are limited to handling assets of persons under the age of 25 years. Custodians hold assets transferred to a minor under the *Uniform Transfers to Minors Act*, discussed in Chapter 3.

CONCLUSION

Be careful. The appointment of your fiduciaries is not to be taken lightly. The best planned will or trust will disintegrate in the hands of an incompetent or dishonest fiduciary. Selecting the best guardian, executor, trustee, or custodian is more important than being concerned over hurting the feelings of a friend or family member.

EXECUTING YOUR WILL 6

You have selected the will form that applies to your situation and filled in all blanks except your signature. You want to legally execute your will by signing your name to it. This chapter will explain what formalities are required to legally execute your will. This chapter discusses two different sets of formalities in executing your will.

SIMPLE EXECUTION

The first set of formalities should be used when you are relatively certain that the provisions of your will are not going to be contested by anyone. This is when your will is relatively consistent with prior wills (if any) and leaves your estate to family members in the proportions they would generally receive by intestate succession (i.e., the distribution of your estate if you have no will).

The following steps can be used when no contest of your will is anticipated.

Step One. You, as the testator announce, in the presence of two competent, adult witnesses who are not beneficiaries or relatives of beneficiaries of the will, that you have read the will, understand the provisions of the will, and that the will disposes of your property in the manner that you want.

Example: "This is my Will. I have read it; I understand it; and, it disposes of my property in a manner that I want of the time of my death."

NOTE: *Keep all persons who benefit from your will or who assisted you in the preparation of your will away from the actual signing of your will, in order to avoid the appearance of undue influence or duress.*

Step Two. In the presence of the two witnesses, sign the will at the end of the signature paragraph (but before the witnesses' signatures) and date the will. The signature paragraph is very short, it simply reads "In Witness hereof, I set my hand hereto on this ____day of _____, 200_" and then has a place for your signature.

Step Three. The witnesses each read the *attestation clause* in the will (right after your signature) and then date and sign their names in the presence of the testator and in the presence of each other. Although not legally required, your witnesses should print their names under their signatures if their handwriting is difficult to read and should also fill-in their addresses.

EXECUTION OF A WILL WHEN CONTEST IS A CONCERN

The second set of formalities should be followed when you believe there could be a contest of the provisions of the will, or when your will does not leave your estate as your family or friends expect it should, or if a person who receives a substantial amount of your estate under your will assists you in the preparation of the will.

Example: There could be a problem if you want to sign a new will leaving everything to your son, who recently moved in with you after he was released from prison, and exclude your other three children. Although you may have excellent and valid reasons for the disposition to your ex-convict son, the will, on the surface, smells "fishy." Such a will, on its surface at least, appears to be the result of duress, fraud, or undue influence of your ex-convict son.

If the disposition of your estate under your will is unusual, or if there could be any allegations concerning your capacity, undue influence, fraud, or duress, then you need extra precautions and help in executing your will.

While Steps One, Two, and Three described previously should still be followed, I strongly recommend that:

- you take your unexecuted will to a lawyer to review and discuss your reasons for the disposition of your estate as directed in your will. Explain in detail why you have directed the disposition as such. Ask the lawyer to make notes and to give you any advice he or she feels appropriate;

- the lawyer you select not be the lawyer of any person who benefits from your will;

- you not permit any person who benefits from your will to make the appointment with the lawyer on your behalf, to accompany you to the lawyer's office, or to be present during your meeting with your lawyer; and,

- you have your lawyer supervise the execution of your will.

ATTESTATION CLAUSE

The attestation clause is the clause right after the signature of the testator (i.e., your signature) and before the signatures of the witnesses. The attestation clause is not required by law. However, the attestation clause has two benefits to the execution of your will.

First, the witnesses "attest" that they know you; they know the document they sign is your will; they saw you sign your will; that you appear to be of sound mind; and, that you do not appear to be under duress or unduly influenced.

Second, the witnesses' statements regarding the execution of the will are stated "under penalty of perjury," which makes the will "self proving" under California law. This permits the court to admit the will to probate after the death of the testator without the testimony of either of the witnesses if the will is uncontested. As it can often be difficult or impossible to locate the witnesses after the death of the testator, the "self proving" attribute of the attestation clauses used in the will forms in this book can be a tremendous benefit.

NOTARIES

Do not use a notary to execute your will. Having a notary verify your signature on your will *instead* of using two witnesses is *not* a proper execution of a will and your will would be invalid.

SIGNING DUPLICATE ORIGINAL WILLS

You may execute more than one original of your will. Duplicate original wills must be signed at the same time, otherwise you simply have a series of the same will, with each successively signed will revoking all of the prior wills. Accordingly, Step One is modified to advise the witnesses that you are signing duplicate wills.

Example: "These two documents are duplicates of my Will. I have read it; I understand it; and, it disposes of my property in a manner that I want it to be disposed of at my death."

Step Two, described previously, is then completed as to all of the duplicate original wills before any of the duplicate original wills are executed by the witnesses in Step Three.

CHANGING AND AMENDING YOUR WILL

7

As your family relationships and estate assets change, you should periodically review and, if necessary, amend your will or execute a new will. Certain events, such as a new marriage or the birth of a child, likely require at least an amendment to your will (called a *codicil*) to avoid the subsequently acquired spouse and child laws described in Chapter 3. This chapter will explain how you can make changes to your will before you execute it and by preparing a separate codicil after you execute your will.

CHANGES BEFORE EXECUTION OF YOUR WILL

When reviewing a will before you sign, it you may find a small error or change you wish to make. For example, the specific cash bequest to your sister is listed as $1,000 and you want to leave her $2,000. The simplest way of correcting or changing your un-executed will may be to simply make a handwritten correction by crossing out the "$1,000" and handwriting in "$2,000" next to the cross-out amount. This is called an *inter-lineation*.

There is always a danger in making a change to your will before you execute it. How is the court supposed to know if you made the change before or after you signed the will? Such a change *before* you sign the will is valid but such a change *after* you sign the will is invalid. To increase the likelihood that the court will determine that your hand-written changes are valid you should date and initial each change as well as have each witness initial the changes *before* you execute the will.

CHANGES AFTER EXECUTION OF YOUR WILL

Often, you want to make changes to your will *after* it has been execut-ed. Do *not* make such changes by crossing out certain parts of the will and/or by inter-lineations, as that method is *not* valid even if you date and initial the changes. After your will is executed you have two choic-es when you want to make changes. First, execute a new will. This is the preferred method if the changes are substantial or if the change may later hurt someone's feeling if they find out.

Example: You want to leave $100 instead of $100,000 to your niece. Consider a new will rather than amending your existing will so that your niece will not know about the prior, larger bequest.

Second, you can execute a separate document amending your will. This might be appropriate if the change is relatively small.

Example: You want to leave $1,000 to your niece who does not receive anything under your will. Consider an amendment to your will.

Amendments to your will are called *codicils*. A codicil adds to your will, subtracts from your will, or simply replaces portions of your existing will. However, a codicil leaves those portions of your will not removed or replaced intact.

Example: Your will names your sister as executor. You execute a codicil naming your brother as alternative executor. Your sister, pur-suant to the will, is still your first appointed executor.

Codicils are executed in the same manner as wills. Form 21, on page 193 in Appendix D is a codicil form.

SAFEKEEPING YOUR WILL 8

Now that you have executed your will, what do you do with the original or duplicate originals? Obviously, you do not place the original will in a location where a person who would benefit if the will was not found after your death has access to it.

Example: Do not leave your will that disinherits your son on the kitchen table when he lives next door. Your son could easily destroy your will and, upon your death, claim his intestate share of your estate.

Generally, a bank safe deposit box is a good location for your will, so long as the safe deposit box is in your name only, or if any co-renter of your safe deposit box has no interest in your will being destroyed. Owning a safe deposit box in your name only does not cause a delay in obtaining your will in the event of your death. Under California Probate Code Section 331, in the event of your death your safe deposit box may be opened for the purpose of the will search. In that event, your safe deposit box is opened in the presence of a bank officer who is required to make a written record of your will, make a copy of your will for their files, and give the original will to your named executor.

If you executed duplicate original wills, you may wish to give one of the duplicate original wills to the named executor or the person who benefits the most under your will.

You should make a couple of copies of your will which you can keep handy for reference. I recommend that you write on the copy where the original will is located.

REVOKING YOUR WILL 9

Things change. Changes in your family relationships or your assets may make your existing will contrary to your current wishes. You can revoke your will in two different ways.

First, you can revoke your will by physically destroying it or by crossing out all of the provisions of the will with the intent to revoke your will. However, *revocation by destruction* is *not* suggested as a court might find that you lacked intent to revoke or that your physically destroyed will was merely "lost." The court might then admit a copy of your revoked will into probate as your final will.

Second, the best way to revoke your will is by executing a new will which states "all prior wills are revoked." All of the forms in this book have the standard "revocation of all prior wills" language in the introductory paragraph. If your new will does not specifically revoke all prior wills, then the prior will remains un-revoked as to matters in it which are not inconsistent with the new will.

Example: The old will leaves Bob $1,000 and the rest to Mary. The new will leaves $5,000 to Ned and the rest to Mary. If the new will does not specifically revoke the old will, Bob still gets his $1,000. If the new will specifically revokes the old will, Bob gets nothing.

In a legal sense, you also revoke at least a portion of your will if you marry or have a child born after you execute your will. Unless your will provides for the after acquired spouse or child, the law "revokes" your will as to the inheritance rights of that spouse or child and he or she receives, from your estate, his or her intestate succession share regardless of what your will says.

ANATOMY OF YOUR WILL 10

This chapter explains the format of the will forms in this book.

Title. The "Last Will and Testament" identifies the document as a will.

Introductory Clause/Revocation of Prior Wills. This paragraph:

- identifies you as the testator of the will;

- declares your county of California residence to assure the county court that it is the proper court of jurisdiction in the event your will needs to be probated after your death; and,

- revokes any and all of your prior wills and codicils. All prior wills and codicils are expressly revoked because your new will does *not* automatically revoke prior wills and codicils. These would have to be read together with your new will if they were not revoked.

Paragraph FIRST. This is a declaration of your marital status and names any predeceased spouse to assist your executor, who must advise the court of the same in the event of the probate of your will. This paragraph lists the names and birth dates of your children to advise the court that you have children, as well as to identify if any children are minors. Also listed are the names of any predeceased children, as well as the names and birth dates of any descendants of predeceased children. These statements assist the executor in giving the required written legal notice to all heirs if the will is filed with the court for probate after your death. The statement "I have no other children or issue of a predeceased child" advises the executor and the court that you have no other issue.

NOTE: *Directive to Pay Debts. A directive to the executor to pay all of your debts adds nothing to the validity or effect of the will. By law, debts must be paid after your death before the bequests are paid. Accordingly, this paragraph is not used in the forms included with this book.*

Paragraph SECOND. This paragraph directs the disposition of your property subject to your will. Most will forms in this book provide separately for bequests of personal property (both tangible and intangible), cash, real property, and the residue of your estate.

Paragraph THIRD. This paragraph provides a comprehensive disinheritance and anti-contest clauses. The *disinheritance clause* states that all persons other than your specifically named beneficiaries are disinherited. If someone shows up after your death claiming to be your long lost brother, he is still subject to the disinheritance clause and receives no part of your estate. However, this clause does not disinherit children born after you execute your will or persons you marry after you execute your will.

The anti-contest clause disinherits anyone who "contests" the will, as well as persons who attempt to contest non-will transfers such as joint tenancies, T.O.D. securities accounts, or life insurance or make claims against your estate for services rendered or under alleged oral agreements to share property. However, the anti-contest clause is only effective against persons who are beneficiaries under the will, as everyone else has already been disinherited under the disinheritance clause.

Paragraph FOURTH. This section nominates the executor of the will and permits the executor to sell property without publishing a written notice of his or her intent to sell the property.

Following paragraph FIFTH is the subscription statement where you date and sign your will.

Paragraph FIFTH. This paragraph explains that all handwritten or typed "fill-ins" in the numbered blanks on your will were made before you executed your will and that all crossed through words and inter-lineations (words written between lines or in the margin) were made before you executed your will and are initialed by you.

Attestation Clause. After your signature is the attestation clause where the witnesses declare, under penalty of perjury, that they witnessed the signing of your will. By making their statement "under penalty of perjury," the court does not require their testimony to prove the validity of your will if its execution is not contested after you die. Your will is considered "self proving." At the end of the attestation clause, the witnesses will each sign his or her name and someone will affix the date.

Guardianship Nomination. If you have minor children and you wish to nominate a guardian to raise them and/or handle their assets, you need to execute one of the two separate forms provided in Appendix D, as that nomination is not included in the will forms.

Glossary

A

administrator.   A personal representative who is not named in the decedent's will. In earlier times, a female administrator was called an administratrix. See also *executor* and *personal representative*.

B

beneficiary.   The named recipient of an asset belonging to a decedent, as distinguished from an "heir."

bequest.   A gift effective at time of death.

bond.   An insurance policy issued to provide financial protection to an estate, a trust, or a custodianship from the dishonest acts of a fiduciary (i.e., an executor, trustee, or custodian).

C

California Probate Code.   A body of written law passed by the legislature that governs the laws and procedures for wills in California.

codicil.   An amendment to a will.

community property.   Property acquired during marriage from the efforts of one or more of the spouses, or property agreed between spouses to be community property (agreement must be in writing if made after 1985). For purposes of inheritance, property acquired outside of California that would have been community property had it been acquired in California, called *quasi-community property* is considered community property. See also *separate property*.

custodian.   A person appointed under the *Uniform Gift to Minors Act* (*Uniform Transfers to Minors Act*), who has a fiduciary position over assets which are for the benefit of a minor or person under the age of 25 years. In essence, a trustee without formal trust documents.

D

decedent.   The person who has died.

devise.   The same as bequest. (California Probate Code uses this term in instead of bequest.)

E

executor.   A personal representative who is named in the decedent's will. In earlier times, a female executor was called an executrix. See also *administrator* and *personal representative*.

execution.   The act of signing a will by the testator and the witnesses.

F

fiduciary.   A term describing a duty to act on behalf of or for another in a fair and trustworthy manner. Also used to describe a person who holds such a duty.

G

guardian.   Person appointed to care for the person and/or the estate of a minor.

H

heir.   The relative entitled to an asset belonging to a decedent when no person is named as the beneficiary. See also *beneficiary*.

holographic will.   A will wherein the essential terms are all in the handwriting of the testator. Although the will must be signed by the testator, the signature need not be at the end of the document, and the will need not be witnessed by any other persons. This type of will is valid in California.

I

inter-lineations.   When one or more words are inserted between the lines or on the margin of a document such as a will.

intestate.   When a person dies without a will.

intestate succession. The distribution of a decedent's property to the decedent's heirs when there is either no will, or the will fails to dispose of the property. In intestate succession:

- if the decedent leaves a surviving spouse, then the community property interest of the decedent passes to the surviving spouse;

- if there is a surviving spouse and no children or other lineal descendants of the decedent, then one-half of the decedent's separate property passes to the surviving spouse and one-half of the decedent's separate property passes to the decedent's family as described below;

- if there is a surviving spouse and one child, then one-half of the separate property passes to the surviving spouse and one-half to the child;

- if there is a surviving spouse and more than one child, then one-third of the separate property passes to the surviving spouse and the remaining separate property passes to the children equally (if any child is deceased but leaves children of his or her own who survive the decedent, then the deceased child's children take their deceased parent's share);

- if there is no surviving spouse, but there are surviving children of the decedent, then they take all of the decedent's separate property, in equal shares;

- if there is no surviving spouse nor issue (children, grandchildren, etc.) who survive, the decedent, then the decedent's separate property, goes to his or her parents, in equal shares or all to the surviving parent; and,

- if there are no surviving parents, then the decedent's separate property passes to the lineal descendants of the decedent's parents (i.e., the siblings of the decedent).

IRC 529 college plan. State-run college education programs permitted by the Internal Revenue Code wherein accounts can be funded by persons for the higher educational benefit of others they select. These programs have substantial federal income tax advantages when the account assets are used for higher educational expenses.

issue. Legal term to describe the lineal descendants of a person. Your issue would be your children, your grandchildren, your great-grandchildren, etc.

J

joint tenancy. A written title naming one or more persons as joint tenants, which means they have equal ownership and, in the event the death of a joint tenant, the remaining joint tenants take the share of the deceased joint tenant "by right of survivorship," regardless of contrary provisions in a will.

L

life estate. The right to use property during your lifetime, but not the right to dispose of the entire property during your life or any of the property at your death.

living trust. A trust created during lifetime (instead of created at someone's death via their will). Generally the trust is for the benefit of the person who creates the trust, but it becomes irrevocable upon the death of the person who creates the trust.

M

minor. Someone under the age of 18 years.

P

personal property. Anything that is not real property. For example: cash, securities, partnership interests, rights in a lawsuit, household furniture and furnishings and personal effects.

personal representative. The generic term for the court appointed person or corporation who manages a decedent's probate estate.

probate. The court supervision of the changing of title to assets from a decedent's name to the name of the beneficiaries under the decedent's will or the decedent's heirs if the decedent died with no will.

Q

quasi-community property. See *community property*.

R

real property. Land, buildings on land, long-term leases, mineral rights, condominiums and co-op buildings (condos where the ownership is indicated by a certificate rather than a deed).

remainderman.   Person who takes the property after the life usage of the property by another. For example, if the testator bequeaths a life estate in his residence to Bob, and then at Bob's death the residence passes to Mary, then Mary is the *remainderman*.

residue.   Those assets of an estate or a will that are left over after the distribution of all specific bequests.

right of representation.   To take the place, for inheritance purposes, of a deceased ancestor. For example, if a will leaves a testator's estate to "my issue by right of representation" and the testator leaves two living children and one deceased child who left two children of his or her own, then the estate would go one-third to each of the living children of the testator and one-sixth to each of the children of the deceased child of the testator.

S

separate property.   Property acquired before marriage, property acquired after marriage by gifts or inheritances, and property agreed upon by the spouses to be separate property (agreement must be in writing if made after 1985). Income earned on separate property without substantial efforts or labor of the spouse owning the separate property is also separate property. See also *community property*.

subscribed will.   A will that is signed by the testator at the end of the document and then signed by at least two witnesses.

T

testamentary capacity.   The legal and mental capacity to execute a will. Generally defined as being 18 years of age or older and aware of one's assets, one's relatives, and knowledge that document takes effect at time of death.

testate.   When a person dies with a will (a person who dies without a will is said to have died "intestate").

testator.   The person whose will we are referring to.

trust.   A legal entity and relationship wherein one person or entity holds legal title and responsibility to property for the financial benefit of another person or entity.

trustee.   Person who holds "title" to the trust assets for the benefit of the beneficiary of the trust. A trustee is responsible for managing the trust assets and has a fiduciary relationship to the beneficiaries of the trust.

W

will.   A document that, at someone's death, directs the distribution of his or her assets. A will generally cannot affect the distribution of assets held in joint tenancy, distributed pursuant to a contract (life insurance, pensions, retirement plans, annuities, etc.), or property subject to a "payable on death" or "transfer on death" designation.

witness.   A person who sees a testator sign his or her will and signs the will after the testator. A witness must be eighteen years or older, aware that the document he or she is signing is a will, and not a beneficiary under the will who takes any more than he or she would have under intestate succession.

CIVIL CODE

28. "Community property" means:

(a) Community property heretofore or hereafter acquired during
marriage by a married person while domiciled in this state.

(b) All personal property wherever situated, and all real property situated in this state, heretofore or hereafter acquired during the marriage by a married person while domiciled elsewhere, that is community property, or a substantially equivalent type of marital property, under the laws of the place where the acquiring spouse was domiciled at the time of its acquisition.

(c) All personal property wherever situated, and all real property situated in this state, heretofore or hereafter acquired during the marriage by a married person in exchange for real or personal property, wherever situated, that is community property, or a substantially equivalent type of marital property, under the laws of the place where the acquiring spouse was domiciled at the time the property so exchanged was acquired.

66. "Quasi-community property" means the following property, other than community property as defined in Section 28:

(a) All personal property wherever situated, and all real property situated in this state, heretofore or hereafter acquired by a decedent while domiciled elsewhere that would have been the community property of the decedent and the surviving spouse if the decedent had been domiciled in this state at the time of its acquisition.

(b) All personal property wherever situated, and all real property situated in this state, heretofore or hereafter acquired in exchange for real or personal property, wherever situated, that would have been the community property of the decedent and the surviving spouse if the decedent had been domiciled in this state at the time the property so exchanged was acquired.

683.

(a) A joint interest is one owned by two or more persons in equal shares, by a title created by a single will or transfer, when expressly declared in the will or transfer to be a joint tenancy, or by transfer from a sole owner to himself or herself and others, or from tenants in common or joint tenants to themselves or some of them, or to themselves or any of them and others, or from a husband and wife, when holding title as community property or otherwise to themselves or to themselves and others or to one of them and to another or others, when expressly declared in the transfer to be a joint tenancy, or when granted or devised to executors or trustees as joint tenants. A joint tenancy in personal property may be created by a written transfer, instrument, or agreement.

(b) Provisions of this section do not apply to a joint account in a financial institution if Part 2 (commencing with Section 5100) of Division 5 of the Probate Code applies to such account.

PROBATE CODE

330.

(a) Except as provided in subdivision (b), a public administrator, government official, law enforcement agency, the hospital or institution in which a decedent died, or the decedent's employer, may, without the need to wait 40 days after death, deliver the tangible personal property of the decedent in its possession, including keys to the decedent's residence, to the decedent's surviving spouse, relative, or conservator or guardian of the estate acting in that capacity at the time of death.

(b) A person shall not deliver property pursuant to this section if the person knows or has reason to believe that there is a dispute over the right to possession of the property.

(c) A person that delivers property pursuant to this section shall require reasonable proof of the status and identity of the person to whom the property is delivered, and may rely on any document described in subdivision (d) of Section 13104 as proof of identity.

(d) A person that delivers property pursuant to this section shall, for a period of three years after the date of delivery of the property, keep a record of the property delivered and the status and identity of the person to whom the property is delivered.

(e) Delivery of property pursuant to this section does not determine ownership of the property or confer any greater rights in the property than the recipient would otherwise have and does not preclude later proceedings for administration of the decedent's estate. If proceedings for administration of the decedent's estate are commenced, the person holding the property shall deliver it to the personal representative on request by the personal representative.

(f) A person that delivers property pursuant to this section is not liable for loss or damage to the property caused by the person to whom the property is delivered.

331.

(a) This section applies only to a safe deposit box in a financial institution held by the decedent in the decedent's sole name, or held by the decedent and others where all are deceased. Nothing in this section affects the rights of a surviving co-holder.

(b) A person who has a key to the safe deposit box may, before letters have been issued, obtain access to the safe deposit box only for the purposes specified in this section by providing the financial institution with both of the following:

(1) Proof of the decedent's death. Proof shall be provided by a certified copy of the decedent's death certificate or by a written statement of death from the coroner, treating physician, or hospital or institution where the decedent died.

(2) Reasonable proof of the identity of the person seeking access. Reasonable proof of identity is provided for the purpose of this paragraph if the requirements of Section 13104 are satisfied.

(c) The financial institution has no duty to inquire into the truth of any statement, declaration, certificate, affidavit, or document offered as proof of the decedent's death or proof of identity of the person seeking access.

(d) When the person seeking access has satisfied the requirements of subdivision (b), the financial institution shall do all of the following:

(1) Keep a record of the identity of the person.

(2) Permit the person to open the safe deposit box under the supervision of an officer or employee of the financial institution, and to make an inventory of its contents.

(3) Make a photocopy of all wills and trust instruments removed from the safe deposit box, and keep the photocopy in the safe deposit box until the contents of the box are removed by the personal representative of the estate or other legally authorized person. The financial institution may charge the person given access a reasonable fee for photocopying.

(4) Permit the person given access to remove instructions for the disposition of the decedent's remains, and, after a photocopy is made, to remove the wills and trust instruments.

(e) The person given access shall deliver all wills found in the safe deposit box to the clerk of the superior court and mail or deliver a copy to the person named in the will as executor or beneficiary as provided in Section 8200.

(f) Except as provided in subdivision (d), the person given access shall not remove any of the contents of the decedent's safe deposit box.

3900. This part may be cited as the "California Uniform Transfers to Minors Act."

3901. In this part:

(a) "Adult" means an individual who has attained the age of 18 years.

(b) "Benefit plan" means an employer's plan for the benefit of an employee or partner.

(c) "Broker" means a person lawfully engaged in the business of effecting transactions in securities or commodities for the person's own account or for the account of others.

(d) "Conservator" means a person appointed or qualified by a court to act as general, limited, or temporary guardian of a minor's property or a person legally authorized to perform substantially the same functions.

(e) "Court" means the superior court.

(f) "Custodial property" means (1) any interest in property transferred to a custodian under this part and (2) the income from and proceeds of that interest in property.

(g) "Custodian" means a person so designated under Section 3909 or a successor or substitute custodian designated under Section 3918.

(h) "Financial institution" means a bank, trust company, savings institution, or credit union, chartered and supervised under state or federal law or an industrial loan company licensed and supervised under the laws of this state.

(i) "Legal representative" means an individual's personal representative or conservator.

(j) "Member of the minor's family" means the minor's parent, stepparent, spouse, grandparent, brother, sister, uncle, or aunt, whether of the whole or half blood or by adoption.

(k) "Minor" means:

(1) Except as provided in paragraph (2), an individual who has not attained the age of 18 years.

(2) When used with reference to the beneficiary for whose benefit custodial property is held or is to be held, an individual who has not attained the age at which the custodian is required under Sections 3920 and 3920.5 to transfer the custodial property to the beneficiary.

(l) "Person" means an individual, corporation, organization, or other legal entity.

(m) "Personal representative" means an executor, administrator, successor personal representative, or special administrator of a decedent's estate or a person legally authorized to perform substantially the same functions.

(n) "State" includes any state of the United States, the District of Columbia, the Commonwealth of Puerto Rico, and any territory or possession subject to the legislative authority of the United States.

(o) "Transfer" means a transaction that creates custodial property under Section 3909.

(p) "Transferor" means a person who makes a transfer under this part.

(q) "Trust company" means a financial institution, corporation, or other legal entity, authorized to exercise general trust powers.

3902.

(a) This part applies to a transfer that refers to this part in the designation under subdivision (a) of Section 3909 by which the transfer is made if at the time of the transfer, the transferor, the minor, or the custodian is a resident of this state or the custodial property is located in this state. The custodianship so created remains subject to this part despite a subsequent change in residence of a transferor, the minor, or the custodian, or the removal of custodial property from this state.

(b) A person designated as custodian under this part is subject to personal jurisdiction in this state with respect to any matter relating to the custodianship.

(c) A transfer that purports to be made and which is valid under the Uniform Transfers to Minors Act, the Uniform Gifts to Minors Act, or a substantially similar

act, of another state is governed by the law of the designated state and may be executed and is enforceable in this state if at the time of the transfer, the transferor, the minor, or the custodian is a resident of the designated state or the custodial property is located in the designated state.

3903.

(a) A person having the right to designate the recipient of property transferable upon the occurrence of a future event may revocably nominate a custodian to receive the property for a minor beneficiary upon the occurrence of the event by naming the custodian followed in substance by the words: "as custodian for (Name of Minor) under the California Uniform Transfers to Minors Act." The nomination may name one or more persons as substitute custodians to whom the property must be transferred, in the order named, if the first nominated custodian dies before the transfer or is unable, declines, or is ineligible to serve. The nomination may be made in a will, a trust, a deed, an instrument exercising a power of appointment, or in a writing designating a beneficiary of contractual rights which is registered with or delivered to the payor, issuer, or other obligor of the contractual rights.

(b) A custodian nominated under this section must be a person to whom a transfer of property of that kind may be made under subdivision (a) of Section 3909.

(c) The nomination of a custodian under this section does not create custodial property until the nominating instrument becomes irrevocable or a transfer to the nominated custodian is completed under Section 3909. Unless the nomination of a custodian has been revoked, upon the occurrence of the future event, the custodianship becomes effective, and the custodian shall enforce a transfer of the custodial property pursuant to Section 3909.

3904.
A person may make a transfer by irrevocable gift to, or the irrevocable exercise of a power of appointment in favor of, a custodian for the benefit of a minor pursuant to Section 3909.

3905.

(a) A personal representative or trustee may make an irrevocable transfer pursuant to Section 3909 to a custodian for the benefit of a minor as authorized in the governing will or trust.

(b) If the testator or settlor has nominated a custodian under Section 3903 to receive the custodial property, the transfer shall be made to that person.

(c) If the testator or settlor has not nominated a custodian under Section 3903, or all persons so nominated as custodian die before the transfer or are unable, decline, or are ineligible to serve, the personal representative or the trustee, as the case may be, shall designate the custodian from among those eligible to serve as custodian for property of that kind under subdivision (a) of Section 3909.

3909.
(a) Custodial property is created and a transfer is made whenever any of the following occurs:

(1) An uncertificated security or a certificated security in registered form is either:

(A) Registered in the name of the transferor, an adult other than the transferor, or a trust company, followed in substance by the words: "as custodian for (Name of Minor) under the California Uniform Transfers to Minors Act."

(B) Delivered if in certificated form, or any document necessary for the transfer of an uncertificated security is delivered, together with any necessary endorsement to an adult other than the transferor or to a trust company as custodian, accompanied by an instrument in substantially the form set forth in subdivision (b).

(2) Money is paid or delivered, or a security held in the name of a broker, financial institution, or its nominee is transferred, to a broker or financial institution for credit to an account in the name of the transferor, an adult other than the transferor, or a trust company, followed in substance by the words: "as custodian for (Name of Minor) under the California Uniform Transfers to Minors Act."

(3) The ownership of a life or endowment insurance policy or annuity contract is either:

(A) Registered with the issuer in the name of the transferor, an adult other than the transferor, or a trust company, followed in substance by the words: "as custodian for (Name of Minor) under the California Uniform Transfers to Minors Act."

(B) Assigned in a writing delivered to an adult other than the transferor or to a trust company whose name in the assignment is followed in substance by the words: "as custodian for (Name of Minor) under the California Uniform Transfers to Minors Act."

(4) An irrevocable exercise of a power of appointment or an irrevocable present right to future payment under a contract is the subject of a written notification delivered to the payor, issuer, or other obligor that the right is transferred to the transferor, an adult other than the transferor, or a trust company, whose name in the notification is followed in substance by the words: "as custo-

dian for (Name of Minor) under the California Uniform Transfers to Minors Act."

(5) An interest in real property is recorded in the name of the transferor, an adult other than the transferor, or a trust company, followed in substance by the words: "as custodian for (Name of Minor) under the California Uniform Transfers to Minors Act."

(6) A certificate of title issued by a department or agency of a state or of the United States which evidences title to tangible personal property is either:

(A) Issued in the name of the transferor, an adult other than the transferor, or a trust company, followed in substance by the words: "as custodian for (Name of Minor) under the California Uniform Transfers to Minors Act."

(B) Delivered to an adult other than the transferor or to a trust company, endorsed to that person followed in substance by the words: "as custodian for (Name of Minor) under the California Uniform Transfers to Minors Act."

(7) An interest in any property not described in paragraphs (1) through (6) is transferred to an adult other than the transferor or to a trust company by a written instrument in substantially the form set forth in subdivision (b).

(b) An instrument in the following form satisfies the requirements of subparagraph (B) of paragraph (1) and paragraph (7) of subdivision (a):

"TRANSFER UNDER THE CALIFORNIA UNIFORM TRANSFERS TO MINORS ACT
I, (Name of Transferor or Name and Representative Capacity if a Fiduciary) hereby transfer to ,(Name of Custodian) as custodian for (Name of Minor) under the California Uniform Transfers to Minors Act, the following: (insert a description of the custodial property sufficient to identify it).
Dated: _____   (Signature)
acknowledges receipt of the (Name of Custodian) property described above as custodian for the minor named above under the California Uniform Transfers to Minors Act.
Dated: _____ "   (Signature of Custodian)

(c) A transferor shall place the custodian in control of the custodial property as soon as practicable.

3910. A transfer may be made only for one minor, and only one person may be the custodian. All custodial property held under this part by the same custodian for the benefit of the same minor constitutes a single custodianship.

3912.

(a) A custodian shall do all of the following:

(1) Take control of custodial property.

(2) Register or record title to custodial property if appropriate.

(3) Collect, hold, manage, invest, and reinvest custodial property.

(b) In dealing with custodial property, a custodian shall observe the standard of care that would be observed by a prudent person dealing with property of another and is not limited by any other statute restricting investments by fiduciaries except that:

(1) If a custodian is not compensated for his or her services, the custodian is not liable for losses to custodial property unless they result from the custodian's bad faith, intentional wrongdoing, or gross negligence, or from the custodian's failure to maintain the standard of prudence in investing the custodial property provided in this section.

(2) A custodian, in the custodian's discretion and without liability to the minor or the minor's estate, may retain any custodial property received from a transferor.

(c) A custodian may invest in or pay premiums on life insurance or endowment policies on (1) the life of the minor only if the minor or the minor's estate is the sole beneficiary or (2) the life of another person in whom the minor has an insurable interest only to the extent that the minor, the minor's estate, or the custodian in the capacity of custodian, is the irrevocable beneficiary.

(d) A custodian at all times shall keep custodial property separate and distinct from all other property in a manner sufficient to identify it clearly as custodial property of the minor. Custodial property consisting of an undivided interest is so identified if the minor's interest is held as a tenant in common and is fixed. Custodial property subject to recordation is so identified if it is recorded, and custodial property subject to registration is so identified if it is either registered, or held in an account designated, in the name of the custodian, followed in substance by the words: "as a custodian for (Name of Minor) under the California Uniform Transfers to Minors Act."

(e) A custodian shall keep records of all transactions with respect to custodial property, including information necessary for the preparation of the minor's tax returns, and shall make them available for inspection at reasonable intervals by a parent or legal representative of the minor or by the minor if the minor has attained the age of 14 years.

3913.

(a) A custodian, acting in a custodial capacity, has all the rights, powers, and authority over custodial property that unmarried adult owners have over their own property, but a custodian may exercise those rights, powers, and authority in that capacity only.

(b) This section does not relieve a custodian from liability for breach of Section 3912.

5500.

(a) This part shall be known as and may be cited as the Uniform TOD Security Registration Act.

(b) This part shall be liberally construed and applied to promote its underlying purposes and policy.

(c) The underlying purposes and policy of this act are to (1) encourage development of a title form for use by individuals that is effective, without **probate** and estate administration, for transferring property at death in accordance with directions of a deceased owner of a security as included in the title form in which the security is held and (2) protect issuers offering and implementing the new title form.

(d) Unless displaced by the particular provisions of this part, the principles of law and equity supplement its provisions.

5505. Registration in beneficiary form may be shown by the words "transfer on death" or the abbreviation "TOD," or by the words "pay on death" or the abbreviation "POD," after the name of the registered owner and before the name of a beneficiary.

5506. The designation of a TOD beneficiary on a registration in beneficiary form has no effect on ownership until the owner's death. A registration of a security in beneficiary form may be canceled or changed at any time by the sole owner or all then surviving owners without the consent of the beneficiary.

5507. On death of a sole owner or the last to die of all multiple owners, ownership of securities registered in beneficiary form passes to the beneficiary or beneficiaries who survive all owners. On proof of death of all owners and compliance with any applicable requirements of the registering entity, a security registered in beneficiary form may be reregistered in the name of the beneficiary or beneficiaries who survive the death of all owners. Until division of the security after the death of all owners, multiple beneficiaries surviving the death of all owners hold their interests as tenants in common. If no beneficiary survives the death of all owners, the security belongs to the estate of the deceased sole owner or the estate of the last to die of all multiple owners.

5509.

(a) Any transfer on death resulting from a registration in beneficiary form is effective by reason of the contract regarding the registration between the owner and the registering entity and this part and is not testamentary.

(b) This part does not limit the rights of a surviving spouse or creditors of security owners against beneficiaries and other transferees under other laws of this state.

6110.

(a) Except as provided in this part, a will shall be in writing and satisfy the requirements of this section.

(b) The will shall be signed by one of the following:

(1) By the testator.

(2) In the testator's name by some other person in the testator's presence and by the testator's direction.

(3) By a conservator pursuant to a court order to make a will under Section 2580.

(c) The will shall be witnessed by being signed by at least two persons each of whom (1) being present at the same time, witnessed either the signing of the will or the testator's acknowledgment of the signature or of the will and (2) understand that the instrument they sign is the testator's will.

6401.

(a) As to community property, the intestate share of the surviving spouse is the one-half of the community property that belongs to the decedent under Section 100.

(b) As to quasi-community property, the intestate share of the surviving spouse is the one-half of the quasi-community property that belongs to the decedent under Section 101.

(c) As to separate property, the intestate share of the surviving spouse is as follows:

(1) The entire intestate estate if the decedent did not leave any surviving issue, parent, brother, sister, or issue of a deceased brother or sister.

(2) One-half of the intestate estate in the following cases:

(A) Where the decedent leaves only one child or the issue of one deceased child.

(B) Where the decedent leaves no issue but leaves a parent or parents or their issue or the issue of either of them.

(3) One-third of the intestate estate in the following cases:

(A) Where the decedent leaves more than one child.

(B) Where the decedent leaves one child and the issue of one or
more deceased children.

(C) Where the decedent leaves issue of two or more deceased children.

6402. Except as provided in Section 6402.5, the part of the intestate estate not passing to the surviving spouse under Section 6401, or the entire intestate estate if there is no surviving spouse, passes as follows:

(a) To the issue of the decedent, the issue taking equally if they are all of the same degree of kinship to the decedent, but if of unequal degree those of more remote degree take in the manner provided in Section 240.

(b) If there is no surviving issue, to the decedent's parent or parents equally.

(c) If there is no surviving issue or parent, to the issue of the parents or either of them, the issue taking equally if they are all of the same degree of kinship to the decedent, but if of unequal degree those of more remote degree take in the manner provided in Section 240.

(d) If there is no surviving issue, parent or issue of a parent, but the decedent is survived by one or more grandparents or issue of grandparents, to the grandparent or grandparents equally, or to the issue of such grandparents if there is no surviving grandparent, the issue taking equally if they are all of the same degree of kinship to the decedent, but if of unequal degree those of more remote degree take in the manner provided in Section 240.

(e) If there is no surviving issue, parent or issue of a parent, grandparent or issue of a grandparent, but the decedent is survived by the issue of a predeceased spouse, to such issue, the issue taking equally if they are all of the same degree of kinship to the predeceased spouse, but if of unequal degree those of more remote degree take in the manner provided in Section 240.

(f) If there is no surviving issue, parent or issue of a parent, grandparent or issue of a grandparent, or issue of a predeceased spouse, but the decedent is survived by next of kin, to the next of kin in equal degree, but where there are two or more collateral kindred in equal degree who claim through different ancestors, those who claim through the nearest ancestor are preferred to those claiming through an ancestor more remote.

(g) If there is no surviving next of kin of the decedent and no surviving issue of a predeceased spouse of the decedent, but the decedent is survived by the parents of a predeceased spouse or the issue of such parents, to the parent or parents equally, or to the issue of such parents if both are deceased, the issue taking equally if they are all of the same degree of kinship to the predeceased spouse, but if of unequal degree those of more remote degree take in the manner provided in Section 240.

6402.5.

(a) For purposes of distributing real property under this section if the decedent had a predeceased spouse who died not more than 15 years before the decedent and there is no surviving spouse or issue of the decedent, the portion of the decedent's estate attributable to the decedent's predeceased spouse passes as follows:

(1) If the decedent is survived by issue of the predeceased spouse, to the surviving issue of the predeceased spouse; if they are all of the same degree of kinship to the predeceased spouse they take equally, but if of unequal degree those of more remote degree take in the manner provided in Section 240.

(2) If there is no surviving issue of the predeceased spouse but the decedent is survived by a parent or parents of the predeceased spouse, to the predeceased spouse's surviving parent or parents equally.

(3) If there is no surviving issue or parent of the predeceased spouse but the decedent is survived by issue of a parent of the predeceased spouse, to the surviving issue of the parents of the predeceased spouse or either of them, the issue taking equally if they are all of the same degree of kinship to the predeceased spouse, but if of unequal degree those of more remote degree take in the manner provided in Section 240.

(4) If the decedent is not survived by issue, parent, or issue of a parent of the predeceased spouse, to the next of kin of the decedent in the manner provided in Section 6402.

(5) If the portion of the decedent's estate attributable to the decedent's predeceased spouse would otherwise escheat to the state because there is no kin of the decedent to take under Section 6402, the portion of the decedent's estate attributable to the predeceased spouse passes to the next of kin of the predeceased spouse who shall take in the same manner as the next of kin of the decedent take under Section 6402.

(b) For purposes of distributing personal property under this section if the decedent had a predeceased spouse who died not more than five years before the decedent, and there is no surviving spouse or issue of the decedent, the portion of the decedent's estate attributable to the decedent's predeceased spouse passes as follows:

(1) If the decedent is survived by issue of the predeceased spouse, to the surviving issue of the predeceased spouse; if they are all of the same degree of kinship to the predeceased spouse they take equally, but if of unequal degree those of more remote degree take in the manner provided in Section 240.

(2) If there is no surviving issue of the predeceased spouse but the decedent is survived by a parent or parents of the predeceased spouse, to the predeceased spouse's surviving parent or parents equally.

(3) If there is no surviving issue or parent of the predeceased spouse but the decedent is survived by issue of a parent of the predeceased spouse, to the surviving issue of the parents of the predeceased spouse or either of them, the issue taking equally if they are all of the same degree of kinship to the predeceased spouse, but if of unequal degree those of more remote degree take in the manner provided in Section 240.

(4) If the decedent is not survived by issue, parent, or issue of a parent of the predeceased spouse, to the next of kin of the decedent in the manner provided in Section 6402.

(5) If the portion of the decedent's estate attributable to the decedent's predeceased spouse would otherwise escheat to the state because there is no kin of the decedent to take under Section 6402, the portion of the decedent's estate attributable to the predeceased spouse passes to the next of kin of the predeceased spouse who shall take in the same manner as the next of kin of the decedent take under Section 6402.

(c) For purposes of disposing of personal property under subdivision (b), the claimant heir bears the burden of proof to show the exact personal property to be disposed of to the heir.

(d) For purposes of providing notice under any provision of this code with respect to an estate that may include personal property subject to distribution under subdivision (b), if the aggregate fair market value of tangible and intangible personal property with a written record of title or ownership in the estate is believed in good faith by the petitioning party to be less than ten thousand dollars ($10,000), the petitioning party need not give notice to the issue or next of kin of the predeceased spouse. If the personal property is subsequently determined to have an aggregate fair market value in excess of ten thousand dollars ($10,000), notice shall be given to the issue or next of kin of the predeceased spouse as provided by law.

(e) For the purposes of disposing of property pursuant to subdivision (b), "personal property" means that personal property in which there is a written record of title or ownership and the value of which in the aggregate is ten thousand dollars ($10,000) or more.

(f) For the purposes of this section, the "portion of the decedent' s estate attributable to the decedent's predeceased spouse" means all of the following property in the decedent's estate:

(1) One-half of the community property in existence at the time of the death of the predeceased spouse.

(2) One-half of any community property, in existence at the time of death of the predeceased spouse, which was given to the decedent by the predeceased spouse by way of gift, descent, or devise.

(3) That portion of any community property in which the predeceased spouse had any incident of ownership and which vested in the decedent upon the death of the predeceased spouse by right of survivorship.

(4) Any separate property of the predeceased spouse which came to the decedent by gift, descent, or devise of the predeceased spouse or which vested in the decedent upon the death of the predeceased spouse by right of survivorship.

(g) For the purposes of this section, quasi-community property shall be treated the same as community property.

(h) For the purposes of this section:

(1) Relatives of the predeceased spouse conceived before the decedent's death but born thereafter inherit as if they had been born in the lifetime of the decedent.

(2) A person who is related to the predeceased spouse through two lines of relationship is entitled to only a single share based on the relationship which would entitle the person to the larger share.

6454. For the purpose of determining intestate succession by a person or the person's issue from or through a foster parent or stepparent, the relationship of parent and child exists between that person and the person's foster parent or stepparent if both of the following requirements are satisfied:

(a) The relationship began during the person's minority and continued throughout the joint lifetimes of the person and the person' s foster parent or stepparent.

(b) It is established by clear and convincing evidence that the foster parent or stepparent would have adopted the person but for a legal barrier.

13050.

(a) For the purposes of this part:

(1) Any property or interest or lien thereon which, at the time of the decedent's death, was held by the decedent as a joint tenant, or in which the decedent had a life

or other interest terminable upon the decedent's death, or which was held by the decedent and passed to the decedent's surviving spouse pursuant to Section 13500, shall be excluded in determining the property or estate of the decedent or its value. This excluded property shall include, but not be limited to, property in a trust revocable by the decedent during his or her lifetime.

(2) A multiple-party account to which the decedent was a party at the time of the decedent's death shall be excluded in determining the property or estate of the decedent or its value, whether or not all or a portion of the sums on deposit are community property, to the extent that the sums on deposit belong after the death of the decedent to a surviving party, P.O.D. payee, or beneficiary. For the purposes of this paragraph, the terms "multiple-party account," "party," "P.O.D. payee," and "beneficiary" are defined in Article 2 (commencing with Section 5120) of Chapter 1 of Part 2 of Division 5.

(b) For the purposes of this part, all of the following property shall be excluded in determining the property or estate of the decedent or its value:

(1) Any vehicle registered under Division 3 (commencing with Section 4000) of the Vehicle Code or titled under Division 16.5 (commencing with Section 38000) of the Vehicle Code.

(2) Any vessel numbered under Division 3.5 (commencing with Section 9840) of the Vehicle Code.

(3) Any manufactured home, mobile home, commercial coach, truck camper, or floating home registered under Part 2 (commencing with Section 18000) of Division 13 of the Health and Safety Code.

(c) For the purposes of this part, the value of the following property shall be excluded in determining the value of the decedent's property in this state:

(1) Any amounts due to the decedent for services in the armed forces of the United States.

(2) The amount, not exceeding five thousand dollars ($5,000), of salary or other compensation, including compensation for unused vacation, owing to the decedent for personal services from any employment.

13100. Excluding the property described in Section 13050, if the gross value of the decedent's real and personal property in this state does not exceed one hundred thousand dollars ($100,000) and if 40 days have elapsed since the death of the decedent, the successor of the decedent may, without procuring letters of administration or awaiting probate of the will, do any of the following with respect to one or more particular items of property:

(a) Collect any particular item of property that is money due the decedent.

(b) Receive any particular item of property that is tangible personal property of the decedent.

(c) Have any particular item of property that is evidence of a debt, obligation, interest, right, security, or chose in action belonging to the decedent transferred, whether or not secured by a lien on real property.

13101.

(a) To collect money, receive tangible personal property, or have evidences of a debt, obligation, interest, right, security, or chose in action transferred under this chapter, an affidavit or a declaration under penalty of perjury under the laws of this state shall be furnished to the holder of the decedent's property stating all of the following:

(1) The decedent's name.

(2) The date and place of the decedent's death.

(3) "At least 40 days have elapsed since the death of the decedent, as shown in a certified copy of the decedent's death certificate attached to this affidavit or declaration."

(4) Either of the following, as appropriate:

(A) "No proceeding is now being or has been conducted in California for administration of the decedent's estate."

(B) "The decedent's personal representative has consented in writing to the payment, transfer, or delivery to the affiant or declarant of the property described in the affidavit or declaration."

(5) "The current gross fair market value of the decedent's real and personal property in California, excluding the property described in Section 13050 of the California Probate Code, does not exceed one hundred thousand dollars ($100,000)."

(6) A description of the property of the decedent that is to be paid, transferred, or delivered to the affiant or declarant.

(7) The name of the successor of the decedent (as defined in Section 13006 of the California Probate Code) to the described property.

(8) Either of the following, as appropriate:

(A) "The affiant or declarant is the successor of the decedent (as defined in Section 13006 of the California Probate Code) to the decedent's interest in the described property."

(B) "The affiant or declarant is authorized under Section 13051 of the California Probate Code to act on behalf of the successor of the decedent (as defined in Section 13006 of the California Probate Code) with respect to the decedent's interest in the described property."

(9) "No other person has a superior right to the interest of the decedent in the described property."

(10) "The affiant or declarant requests that the described property be paid, delivered, or transferred to the affiant or declarant."

(11) "The affiant or declarant affirms or declares under penalty of perjury under the laws of the State of California that the foregoing is true and correct."

(b) Where more than one person executes the affidavit or declaration under this section, the statements required by subdivision (a) shall be modified as appropriate to reflect that fact.

(c) If the particular item of property to be transferred under this chapter is a debt or other obligation secured by a lien on real property and the instrument creating the lien has been recorded in the office of the county recorder of the county where the real property is located, the affidavit or declaration shall satisfy the requirements both of this section and of Section 13106.5.

(d) A certified copy of the decedent's death certificate shall be attached to the affidavit or declaration.

(e) If the decedent's personal representative has consented to the payment, transfer, or delivery of the described property to the affiant or declarant, a copy of the consent and of the personal representative's letters shall be attached to the affidavit or declaration.

13500. Except as provided in this chapter, when a husband or wife dies intestate leaving property that passes to the surviving spouse under Section 6401, or dies testate and by his or her will devises all or a part of his or her property to the surviving spouse, the property passes to the survivor subject to the provisions of Chapter 2 (commencing with Section 13540) and Chapter 3 (commencing with Section 13550), and no administration is necessary.

13501. Except as provided in Chapter 6 (commencing with Section 6600) of Division 6 and in Part 1 (commencing with Section 13000) of this division, the following property of the decedent is subject to administration under this **code**:

(a) Property passing to someone other than the surviving spouse under the decedent's will or by intestate succession.

(b) Property disposed of in trust under the decedent's will.

(c) Property in which the decedent's will limits the surviving spouse to a qualified ownership. For the purposes of this subdivision, a devise to the surviving spouse that is conditioned on the spouse surviving the decedent by a specified period of time is not a "qualified ownership" interest if the specified period of time has expired. 21110.

(a) Subject to subdivision (b), if a transferee is dead when the instrument is executed, or fails or is treated as failing to survive the transferor or until a future time required by the instrument, the issue of the deceased transferee take in the transferee's place in the manner provided in Section 240. A transferee under a class gift shall be a transferee for the purpose of this subdivision unless the transferee's death occurred before the execution of the instrument and that fact was known to the transferor when the instrument was executed.

(b) The issue of a deceased transferee do not take in the transferee's place if the instrument expresses a contrary intention or a substitute disposition. A requirement that the initial transferee survive the transferor or survive for a specified period of time after the death of the transferor constitutes a contrary intention. A requirement that the initial transferee survive until a future time that is related to the probate of the transferor's will or administration of the estate of the transferor constitutes a contrary intention.

(c) As used in this section, "transferee" means a person who is kindred of the transferor or kindred of a surviving, deceased, or former spouse of the transferor.

21610. Except as provided in Section 21611, if a decedent fails to provide in a testamentary instrument for the decedent's surviving spouse who married the decedent after the execution of all of the decedent's testamentary instruments, the omitted spouse shall receive a share in the decedent's estate, consisting of the following property in said estate:

(a) The one-half of the community property that belongs to the decedent under Section 100.

(b) The one-half of the quasi-community property that belongs to the decedent under Section 101.

(c) A share of the separate property of the decedent equal in value to that which the spouse would have received if the decedent had died without having executed a testamentary instrument, but in no event is the share to be more than one-half the value of the separate property in the estate.

21611. The spouse shall not receive a share of the estate under Section 21610 if any of the following is established:

(a) The decedent's failure to provide for the spouse in the decedent's testamentary instruments was intentional and that intention appears from the testamentary instruments.

(b) The decedent provided for the spouse by transfer outside of the estate passing by the decedent's testamentary instruments and the intention that the transfer be in lieu of a provision in said instruments is shown by statements of the decedent or from the amount of the transfer or by other evidence.

(c) The spouse made a valid agreement waiving the right to share in the decedent's estate.

21620. Except as provided in Section 21621, if a decedent fails to provide in a testamentary instrument for a child of decedent born or adopted after the execution of all of the decedent's testamentary instruments, the omitted child shall receive a share in the decedent's estate equal in value to that which the child would have received if the decedent had died without having executed any testamentary instrument.

21621. A child shall not receive a share of the estate under Section 21620 if any of the following is established:

(a) The decedent's failure to provide for the child in the decedent's testamentary instruments was intentional and that intention appears from the testamentary instruments.

(b) The decedent had one or more children and devised or otherwise directed the disposition of substantially all the estate to the other parent of the omitted child.

(c) The decedent provided for the child by transfer outside of the estate passing by the decedent's testamentary instruments and the intention that the transfer be in lieu of a provision in said instruments is show by statements of the decedent or from the amount of the transfer or by other evidence.

21622. If, at the time of the execution of all of decedent's testamentary instruments effective at the time of decedent's death, the decedent failed to provide for a living child solely because the decedent believed the child to be dead or was unaware of the birth of the child, the child shall receive a share in the estate equal in value to that which the child would have received if the decedent had died without having executed any testamentary instruments.

Appendix B
Asset Roadmap

Sometimes I am involved in a decedent's estate when no one, not even the decedent's family, has any idea as to what the assets or the estate are or where they should look for the decedent's will and other important papers. In those cases we often find health care powers of attorney after the decedent has died or the decedent's burial instructions after the funeral, when it is too late. To avoid putting your family through such heartache, I suggest that you keep an "asset roadmap" detailing where your important papers are going to be found and listing both your assets as well as the tentative disposition of your assets which pass outside of your will and probate.

The following *Roadmap* should be copied and used by you, from time to time, to update where your family can find your will, powers of attorney for health care and estate manement and location of your safe deposit box, as well as a listing of your life insurance, insurance for your health, you car, and your house. If you want, you can even list where you keep your tax returns and make a suggestion as to what attorney your family should hire to assist them in the event of your death. In addition, there is space to insert, right on the *Roadmap*, a legally binding directive as to your burial or funeral instructions. Finally, the *Roadmap* permits you to list your assets, i.e., your real property, your securities, your bank accounts and any other assets you own.

Instructions:

Will. List the date of your will, where the original is kept, and who the nominated Executor is.

Codicil. List the date of your Codicil and where the original is kept.

Power of Attorney. List the date, location of the original and name of the nominated agent for both your Health Care Power of Attorney and your Power of Attorney for Estate Management. Remember, by law, a copy of your Health Care Power of Attorney has the legal effect of an original.

Safe Deposit Box. List the name and location of the bank, the location of the safe deposit box key, the number of the box, and the names of any "co-renters" of the box.

Life Insurance. List the name of each insurance company, the face amount of the policy, the policy number, the location of the original policy, and the name of the policy beneficiary.

Other Insurance. List the location of your original policies for auto, household, etc.

Burial/Funeral Instructions. You may leave written instructions as to the disposition of your remains. If you have made pre-arrangements or if you own a crypt or plot you should include that information as well as the location of any pre-need contracts or cemetery deeds.

Assets. List all of your *real property, securities, bank accounts, personal property* such as cars and boats and other miscellaneous property.

> **Real Property.** List the location of the property and how you hold title. For example, 20 Maple St., Los Angeles, John Smith and Mary Smith, as joint tenants.

> **Securities.** List all stocks, bonds, and brokerage accounts. As to actual certificates for stocks and bonds, you should list the number of shares under the subheading "Account #." As to brokerage accounts, you do not need to list the individual securities within the account. As with real property, list how the title is held as to each security or brokerage account. If you hold a brokerage account in your name with a "transfer on death" designation, list your name with TOD and the name of the beneficiary in the event of your death.

> **Bank Accounts.** List the name and location of each financial institution, the account numbers, where the bank books or CD certificates are located and the title vesting for each account. For totten trust accounts list your name and then ATF ("as trustee for") and then the name of the beneficiary in the event of your death.

> **Autos/Boats/Etc.** List the location of the certificate of title for each asset. The certificate of title itself will indicate any co-ownership rights.

> **Partnerships/Annuities/Royalties/Misc. Assets.** List the names of assets, location of original documentation of ownership, a description of the assets with any account number, and the name of any beneficiary.

Tax Returns. List where your prior year tax returns can be found.

Lawyer. List the name of any lawyer that either has information concerning any of the above and/or that you would like your family/beneficiaries to contact regarding assistance in the handling of your estate.

ASSET ROADMAP

WILL

Date

Location

Executor

CODICIL

Date

Location

POWER OF ATTORNEY

HEALTH

Date

Location

Agent

FINANCIAL

Date

Location

Agent

SAFE DEPOSIT BOX

Location

Location of Key

Box #

_____

Co-Renter

_____

LIFE INSURANCE

Company

_____

Amount

_____

Policy #

_____

Location

_____

Company

_____

Amount

_____

Policy #

_____

Location

_____

Company

_____

Amount

_____

Policy #

_____

Location

_____

Company

_____

Amount

_____

Policy #

_____

Location

_____

OTHER INSURANCE

Auto
_____

Household
_____

Other
_____

BURIAL/FUNERAL INSTRUCTIONS

_____

_____

_____

ASSETS

REAL PROPERTY
_____

Location
_____

Title
_____

Location
_____

Title
_____

Location
_____

Title
_____

Location
_____

Title
_____

SECURITIES

Name	Account #	Title
1.		
2.		
3.		
4.		
5.		

BANK ACCOUNTS

Location	Account #	Title
1.		
2.		
3.		
4.		
5.		

AUTOS/BOATS/ETC

Description of Auto/Boat/etc.

Location of Title Certificate

Description of Auto/Boat/etc.

Location of Title Certificate

Description of Auto/Boat/etc.

Location of Title Certificate

PARTNERSHIPS/ANNUITIES/ROYALTIES/MISC. INVESTMENTS

1.

2.

3.

TAX RETURNS

Location

LAWYER REFERRAL

Appendix C
Step-By-Step Instructions and Sample Completed Forms

NUMBER KEY

In the forms included in this book the "blanks" to be filled in by you are each numbered. Use the following as a reference guide as to how to complete each blank based upon its assigned number. (Three sample completed forms are located in this section. Use these as models for the blank forms in Appendix D.)

(1): Your name (not your signature).

(2): Name of the county where you live.

(3): State whether you are a widow or unmarried.

(4): Name of your spouse if you are married or a widow. If you are unmarried (never married or divorced) write "Not Applicable."

(5): Name(s) of your child(ren) and their birthdates. If a child is an adult you can simply list his or her name, a comma and the words "an adult." *For example: "Bob Smith, born 12/25/02" or "Mary Lee, an adult."*

(6): Name(s) of the descendants now living of any predeceased children you have. *For example, if your son, Bob, is now deceased, but left two children and one grandchild now living, you would list all three of those descendants of Bob and their relationship to you (i.e., a grandchild, great-grandchild, etc.).* If you have no deceased child who left descendants now surviving, write "Not Applicable."

(7): If you wrote "Not Applicable" for (6) above, insert "Not Applicable." If you have a pre-deceased child(ren) who left descendants now surviving and listed all of the descendants in (6) above you insert "no other."

(8): List all bequests of personal, tangible property like furniture, cars, jewelry, etc. *For example:* "*My green couch to my nephew, Bob Smith.*" If you are not making any specific bequests of personal, tangible property, simply write "Not Applicable."

(9): List who will receive your personal, tangible property that is not specifically disposed of in (8). *For example: "my nephew, Bob Smith" or "my friends, Ned Jones and Mary Lee."* If you want to leave your personal, tangible property to your residual beneficiaries listed in item (18) write "Not Applicable."

(10): List any cash bequests to beneficiaries. *For example: "My nephew, Bob Smith, the cash sum of Ten Thousand Dollars ($10,000.00)."* If you do not wish to make any cash bequests write "Not Applicable."

(11): List any specific bequests of real estate to beneficiaries. *For example: "My nephew, Bob Smith, the residential real property located at 12 Maple Ave., Los Angeles, CA."* If you do not wish to make any specific bequests of real estate write "Not Applicable."

(12): If you do not make any specific bequests of real estate in item (11) you can ignore item (12). If you do make specific bequests of real estate in item (11) you need to either do nothing at item (12) if you want the beneficiary of the real estate to receive the property free of all mortgages and liens. If, however, you want to the bequest of real property to carry with it any mortgage or liens recorded against that property you need to put a line through the sentence after item (12) and place your initials next to the end of the cross out BEFORE you sign your Will.

(13) Name of the "life estate" beneficiary. (If you are not giving someone a life estate in real property do not use this form.)

(14): Location of property subject to the life estate.

(15): Name of person or entity that takes the life estate property after the death of the life estate beneficiary named in (13).

(16) and (17): You are bequeathing the residue of your estate, i.e., everything not already specifically bequeathed. If you are leaving your residue in differing propor-

tions such as 40 shares to Bob and 60 shares (remember to use shares, when possible, instead of percentages to avoid problems when a beneficiary predeceases you) to Mary (or "All" to a single beneficiary) then you will leave the words between items (16) and (17) intact and cross out the words "in equal shares" after item (16) and initial said cross out BEFORE you sign your Will. If, instead you want to leave the residue of your estate to more than one beneficiary, in equal shares, you will cross out the words between item (16) and (17) and initial said cross out BEFORE you sign your Will.

(18): Names of only the beneficiaries of the residue of your estate (if you crossed out the words between item (16) and (17)) or names of the beneficiaries of the residue of your estate and their proportions (if you crossed out the words "in equal shares" after item (17)). *For example: "To my nephew, Bob Smith, 20 shares and to my niece, Mary Lee, 80 shares" or " All to my nephew, Bob Smith."*

(19): The number of shares of the residue of your estate going to the trust created under your will. (If you are not leaving any portion of the residue of your estate to a trust created under your will, you should be using a different form.)

(20): Name of the beneficiary of the trust, that is, the person who receives the income/principal of the trust.

(21): The age at which time the beneficiary receives one-half of his/her trust principal. If you want the beneficiary to receive all of his/her trust principal at one age, write in "N/A" for "Not Applicable" and proceed to item (22).

(22): The age at which time the beneficiary receives the rest (or all) of his/her trust principal. Typically you will separate the ages at which time the beneficiary receives his/her trust principal by five years.

(23): Name of the beneficiary who receives the trust estate after the death of the life beneficiary of the trust.

(24): Name of the beneficiary who receives the trust estate after the death of the life beneficiary, if the beneficiary in item (23) is then deceased. If no such beneficiary is to be named in item (23) write "Not Applicable."

(25) Name of the person or entity who acts as the trustee. You can nominate two Trustees.

(26) Insert "co" before the word "trustee" and an "s" at the end of the word trustee if you nominate more than one trustee at item (25). If you nominate one trustee at item (25) do nothing at item (26).

(27) Do nothing if you want the trustee you nominated to act without posting a surety bond. Cross out the words "without bond" and initial said cross out if you want your trustee to post a surety bond (recommended). *Reminder: Corporate Trustees do not have to post bonds.*

(28) Name of the person or entity who is to act as the back-up trustee.

(29) The age (anywhere from 18 years to 25 years) that the beneficiary will receive his or her custodial property.

(30) Name of the person or entity who is to act as custodian. *You cannot nominate co-custodians.*

(31) Identify which codicil you are preparing. Is it the first codicil to your will or the second, etc., codicil?

(32) Do nothing if you want the custodian(s) you nominated to act without posting a surety bond. Cross out the words "without bond" and initial said cross out if you want your Custodian to post a surety bond (recommended). *Reminder: Corporate Custodians do not have to post bonds.*

(33) Name of the person or entity who is to act as the back-up custodian.

(34): Name of the person or entity who is to act as your executor. *You can nominate two executors.*

(35) Insert "co" before the word "executor" and an "s" at the end of the word executor if you nominate more than one executor in item (34). If you nominate one executor at item (34) do nothing at item (35).

(36): Do nothing if you want your executor to act without posting a surety bond. Cross out the words "without bond" and initial said cross out if you want your Executor to post a surety bond (recommended). *Reminder: Corporate Executors do not have to post bonds.*

(37): Name of the person or entity who is to act as the back-up executor.

(38): Insert the date.

(39): Insert the name of the city where your will is being signed.

(40): Sign your name.

(41): First witness signs his or her name.

(42): First witness writes his or her address.

(43): Second witness signs his or her name.

(44): Second witness writes his or her address.

(45): Insert date of will you are amending

(46): Insert amendment words. *For example: "I married Sue Smith on August 1, 2003."*

(47): You must select either Option 1 or Option 2. If you select Option 1, then you must cross through the words between (47 - Option 2 Start) and (47 - Option 2B End) AND place your initials in the margin near the crossed through words.

If you select Option 2, cross through the words between (47 - Option 1 Start) and (47 - Option 1 End) AND either cross through the words between (47 - Option 2A End) and (47 - Option 2B Start) OR cross through the words between (47 - Option 2B Start) and (47 - Option 2B End), depending on your selections. *Remember: Initial on the margin next to the crossed through words.*

Sample Forms

form 3: Last Will and Testament—*All to spouse, then all to children, with guardianship*

form 8: Last Will and Testament—*To spouse with trust for one or more adult children*

form 15: Last Will and Testament—*No spouse or children, create a life estate for someone*

LAST WILL AND TESTAMENT

I, (1)__ROBERT SMITH_____, a resident of (2)_LOS ANGELES____ County, California, being of sound and disposing mind and memory and not acting under duress, menace, fraud or undue influence of any person whomsoever, do make, publish and declare this to be my Last Will and Testament, and I hereby expressly revoke all other wills, codicils, and testamentary writings heretofore made by me.

FIRST.   I declare that I am married. My spouse's name is (4)__MARTHA SMITH_____. I have the following children:

(5) MARY SMITH, BORN 3/1/98; AND

TOM SMITH, BORN 7/2/00

I have a deceased child who left the following issue now surviving:

(6) NOT APPLICABLE

I have no other children and (7) NOT APPLICABLE deceased children who left issue now surviving.

SECOND. I devise all of estate to my spouse. In the event my spouse should predecease me then I leave all of my estate to my issue, by right of representation.

THIRD: I have intentionally and with full knowledge omitted to provide for my issue, ancestors, relatives and heirs living at the time of my demise, except for such provisions as are made specifically herein.

If any person who is or claims under or through a beneficiary of this Will, or if any person who would be entitled to share in my estate if I died intestate, should in any manner whatsoever, directly or indirectly, attack, contest or seek to impair or invalidate in court any provision of the following:

A. This Will or any Codicil to this Will;

B. Any revocable or irrevocable Trust established by me;

C. Any beneficiary designation executed by me with respect to any insurance policy, any "totten trust" account, any joint tenancy, any "transfer on death" account or any pension plan, or conspire or cooperate with anyone attempting to do any of the actions or things aforesaid, then I hereby specifically disinherit each such person and any devise, share or interest in my estate otherwise given to each such person under this Will or to which each such person might be entitled by law, is hereby revoked and shall pass and be distributed as though each such person had predeceased me leaving no issue or heirs whatsoever.

Any and every individual who asserts, or conspires or cooperates with any person who asserts, any claim against my Estate based on:

D. "Quantum meruit" theory;

E. Common law marriage, Marvin v. Marvin, 18 Cal. 3d 660 (1976) type of agreement or similar theory;

F. Constructive trust theory; or,

G. Oral agreement or written agreement which is to be proved by parole evidence, claiming that I agreed to gift or devise anything to such person or to pay such person or another for services rendered, regardless of whether a court may find that such agreement existed, then I hereby specifically disinherit each such person and any devise, share or interest in my estate otherwise given to each such person under this Will or to which each such person might be entitled by law, is hereby revoked and shall pass and be distributed as though each such person had predeceased me leaving no issue or heirs whatsoever.

FOURTH: I nominate and appoint my spouse as Executor hereunder without bond. In the event my spouse should decline, become unable or, for any reason, cease to serve as Executor then I nominate and appoint (37) _BILL E. SMITH_ as Executor hereunder (36) without bond.

I authorize my Executor to sell, at either public or private sale, encumber or lease any property belonging to my estate, either with or without public notice, subject to such confirmation as may be required by law, and to hold, manage and operate any such property.

FIFTH. All typed and handwritten "fill-ins" where directed above were made before the execution of this Will and are not initialed by me. All crossed through words and inter-lineations were made before the execution of this Will and are initialed by me.

Except as provided otherwise herein, the masculine, feminine, and neuter gender and the singular or plural number, shall each be deemed to include the others whenever the context so indicates.

IN WITNESS WHEREOF, I have hereunto set my hand this (38)_JANUARY 31, 2003_ at (39) _GLENDALE_, CA.

(40)_Robert Smith_

The foregoing instrument, consisting of four pages, including the page on which this attestation clause is completed and signed, was at the date hereof by (1)_ROBERT SMITH_ signed as and declared to be his/her Will, in the presence of us who, at his/her request and in his/her presence, and in the presence of each other, have subscribed our names as witnesses thereto. Each of us observed the signing of this Will by (1)_ROBERT SMITH_ and by each other subscribing witness and knows that each signature is the true signature of the person whose name was signed.

Each of us is now an adult and a competent witness and resides at the address set forth after his or her name.

We are acquainted with (1) ROBERT SMITH . At this time, he/she is over the age of eighteen years, and to the best of our knowledge, he/she is of sound mind and is not acting under duress, menace, fraud, misrepresentation, or undue influence.

We declare under penalty of perjury that the foregoing is true and correct.

Executed on (38) JANUARY 31, 2003 at (39) GLENDALE , CA.

(41) *Mabel Jones*

                             Residing at (42) 555 MAIN ST.,

                             EAGLE ROCK, CA

(43) *Ralph Jones*

                             Residing at (44) 555 MAIN ST.

                             EAGLE ROCK, CA

LAST WILL AND TESTAMENT

I, (1) ROBERT SMITH   , a resident of (2) LOS ANGELES   County, California, being of sound and disposing mind and memory and not acting under duress, menace, fraud or undue influence of any person whomsoever, do make, publish and declare this to be my Last Will and Testament, and I hereby expressly revoke all other wills, codicils, and testamentary writings heretofore made by me.

FIRST.   I declare that I am married. My spouse's name is (4) MARTHA SMITH   . I have the following children:

(5) ANDREW SMITH, BORN 10/03/88; AND,

   ALISON SMITH, BORN 5/18/90

I have a deceased child who left the following issue now surviving:

(6) MIKE SMITH

I have no other children and (7) NOT APPLICABLE deceased children who left issue now surviving.

SECOND. I devise the following personal, tangible property:

(8) MY MORRIS MINOR CAR TO MY BROTHER, BILLY SMITH

I devise to (9) MARTHA SMITH AND ANDREW SMITH   all of my remaining personal effects, household furniture and furnishings, trailers, boats, pictures, works of art and art objects, collections, jewelry, silverware, wearing apparel, collections, sporting goods, and all other articles of household or personal use or ornament at whatsoever time acquired by me and wheresoever situated.

I devise to the following persons the cash amount listed after their respective names:

(10) `ALISON SMITH, TEN THOUSAND DOLLARS ($10,000.00)`

I devise to the following persons the real property described after their respective names. (12) Said real property is given free of all encumbrances or liens thereon.

(11) `MY RESIDENCE LOCATED AT 24 TINDAYA, GLENDALE, TO MY WIFE, MARTHA SMITH`

In the event any of the above named persons should predecease me or fail to survive me then his or her share shall lapse unless I have specifically named a person to take said bequest in the event of the first beneficiary's death.

Any beneficiary above who fails to survive me by thirty days shall be deemed to have predeceased me.

I devise all of the rest, residue and remainder of my estate, real, personal and mixed, of whatsoever kind or character and wheresoever situated, of which I die possessed or to which I may in any manner be entitled, to the following persons or entities (16) in the proportions listed after their names (17) in equal shares.

(18) `MARTHA SMITH, 80 SHARES; AND`

`MIKE SMITH, 1 SHARE`

(19)_19_ shares to the Trustee hereinafter named, to have and to hold for the benefit of (20)ANDREW SMITH_____upon the uses, trusts, purposes and conditions hereinafter provided.   1. If the beneficiary, his or her spouse, or any of his children should at any time or from time to time be in need, in the discretion of the Trustee, of funds due to illness, infirmity or other physical or mental disability or any emergency, the Trustee may relieve or contribute toward the relief of any such need or needs of the beneficiary by paying to him or her or using and applying for his or her benefit, such sum or sums out of the income and/or principal of his or her trust as the Trustee, in the Trustee's discretion, may deem necessary or advisable.

2. The Trustee shall pay the beneficiary all of the net income, in monthly or other convenient installments, from the trust.

3.a. (47 - Option 1 Start) Upon the beneficiary attaining the age of (21)_25_ years, the Trustee shall distribute and deliver to such beneficiary one-half of his trust estate. Upon each beneficiary attaining the age of (22)_30_ years, the Trustee shall distribute and deliver to such beneficiary all of the remainder of his or her trust estate.

3.b. If, upon the attaining of the above ages, the Trustee suspects that said beneficiary may be abusing drugs and/or alcohol, the Trustee may require the beneficiary to take a reasonable drug and/or alcohol test. If the beneficiary fails said test, the trustee shall defer said principal payment to the beneficiary until the beneficiary passes said test. After a failed test, subsequent drug tests shall be administered at the request of the beneficiary but not less than six months after a prior test. In the event a beneficiary fails a drug and/or alcohol test, the Trustee may use said beneficiary's trust estate to pay for a drug and/or alcohol abuse rehabilitation program and may require the beneficiary to enroll and to complete said program as a condition precedent to the taking of a subsequent drug and/or alcohol test.

3.c. In the event the beneficiary should die before complete distribution to him or her of his or her trust estate, his or her entire trust estate on hand at the time of his death shall thereupon be apportioned and distributed to his or her surviving issue, by right of representation. If such beneficiary should die before complete distribution to him or her of his or her trust estate and leave no surviving issue, then the balance of the trust estate then on hand shall go and be distributed to my heirs to be determined according to the laws of the State of California then in effect relating to the intestate succession of separate property not acquired from a predeceased spouse. (47 - Option 1 End)

~~OR~~

~~3.a. (47 - Option 2 Start) In addition to any other payments to the beneficiary hereunder, the Trustee shall, upon the written request of the beneficiary in December of each calendar year, pay to the beneficiary amounts from principal that the beneficiary requests, not exceeding in any single calendar year the greater of the following amounts: $5,000.00 or 5 percent of the value of the principal of the beneficiary's trust estate; determined as of the end of the calendar year. This right of withdrawal is noncumulative, so that if the beneficiary does not withdraw the full amount permitted to be withdrawn during any calendar year, the right to withdraw the remaining amount will lapse at the end of the calendar year.~~

~~3.b. On the death of the beneficiary his or her entire trust estate on hand at the time of his death shall thereupon be apportioned and distributed to (23)_____. If (23)_____ is then deceased then the trust estate then on hand shall go to (24)_____, if he is then living. (47 - Option 2A End)~~

~~OR:~~

~~the beneficiary's surviving issue, by right of representation. If such beneficiary should die before complete distribution to him or her of his or her trust estate and leave no surviving issue, then the balance of the trust estate then on hand shall go and be distributed to my heirs to be determined according to the laws of the State of California then in effect relating to the intestate succession of separate property not acquired from a predeceased spouse. (47 - Option 2B End)~~ *RS*

4. Each beneficiary hereunder is hereby prohibited from anticipating, encumbering, assigning, or in any other manner alienating his or her interest in either income or principal, and is without power so to do, nor shall such interest be subject to his or her liabilities or obligations, nor to attachment, execution, or other legal processes, bankruptcy proceedings or claims of creditors or others. The Trustee may, however, deposit in any bank designated in writing by a beneficiary, to his or her credit, income or principal payable to such beneficiary.

5. If, at any time, a trust created hereunder shall, in the sole judgment of the Trustee, be of the aggregate principal value of Fifty Thousand Dollars ($50,000.00) or less, the Trustee may, but need not, terminate such trust and distribute the assets thereof in the Trustee's possession to the beneficiary or beneficiaries, at the time of the current income

thereof, and if there is more than one beneficiary, in the proportion in which they are beneficiaries.

6. I nominate and appoint (25) <u>MARTHA SMITH</u> as (26) <u>Not Applicable</u>
Trustee hereunder (27) without bond. In the event he/she or both of them should die,
decline to act, or for any other reason, be unable to act as Trustee then I appoint (28)
<u>BILLY SMITH</u> as Trustee hereunder (27) without bond.

THIRD: I have intentionally and with full knowledge omitted to provide for my issue, ancestors, relatives and heirs living at the time of my demise, except for such provisions as are
made specifically herein.

If any person who is or claims under or through a beneficiary of this Will, or if any
person who would be entitled to share in my estate if I died intestate, should in any manner
whatsoever, directly or indirectly, attack, contest or seek to impair or invalidate in court any
provision of the following:

A. This Will or any Codicil to this Will;

B. Any revocable or irrevocable Trust established by me;

C. Any beneficiary designation executed by me with respect to any insurance policy, any "totten trust" account, any joint tenancy, any "transfer on death" account or any pension plan,

or conspire or cooperate with anyone attempting to do any of the actions or things aforesaid,
then I hereby specifically disinherit each such person and any devise, share or interest in my
estate otherwise given to each such person under this Will or to which each such person
might be entitled by law, is hereby revoked and shall pass and be distributed as though each
such person had predeceased me leaving no issue or heirs whatsoever.

Any and every individual who asserts, or conspires or cooperates with any person who
asserts, any claim against my Estate based on:

D. "Quantum meruit" theory;

E. Common law marriage, Marvin v. Marvin, 18 Cal. 3d 660 (1976) type of agreement or
similar theory;

F. Constructive trust theory; or,

G. Oral agreement or written agreement which is to be proved by parole evidence, claiming that I agreed to gift or devise anything to such person or to pay such person or another for services rendered, regardless of whether a court may find that such agreement existed,

then I hereby specifically disinherit each such person and any devise, share or interest in my estate otherwise given to each such person under this Will or to which each such person might be entitled by law, is hereby revoked and shall pass and be distributed as though each such person had predeceased me leaving no issue or heirs whatsoever.

FOURTH: I nominate and appoint (34) <u>MARTHA SMITH AND BILLY SMITH</u> as (35) <u>CO</u>-ExecutorS hereunder (36) without bond. In the event he/she or both of them should decline, become unable or, for any reason, cease to serve as Executor then I nominate and appoint (37) <u>BRIAN HOPP</u> as Executor hereunder (36) without bond.

I authorize my Executor to sell, at either public or private sale, encumber or lease any property belonging to my estate, either with or without public notice, subject to such confirmation as may be required by law, and to hold, manage and operate any such property.

FIFTH. All handwritten "fill-ins" where directed above were made before the execution of this Will and are not initialed by me. All inter-lineations were made before the execution of this Will and are initialed by me.

The masculine, feminine, and neuter gender and the singular or plural number, shall each be deemed to include the others whenever the context so indicates.

IN WITNESS WHEREOF, I have hereunto set my hand this

(38) <u>JANUARY 31, 2003</u> at (39) <u>GLENDALE</u>, CA.

(40) *Robert Smith*

The foregoing instrument, consisting of seven pages, including the page on which this attestation clause is completed and signed, was at the date hereof by (1) ROBERT SMITH signed as and declared to be his/her Will, in the presence of us who, at his/her request and in his/her presence, and in the presence of each other, have subscribed our names as witnesses thereto. Each of us observed the signing of this Will by (1) ROBERT SMITH and by each other subscribing witness and knows that each signature is the true signature of the person whose name was signed.

Each of us is now an adult and a competent witness and resides at the address set forth after his or her name.

We are acquainted with (1) ROBERT SMITH . At this time, he/she is over the age of eighteen years, and to the best of our knowledge, he/she is of sound mind and is not acting under

duress, menace, fraud, misrepresentation, or undue influence.

We declare under penalty of perjury that the foregoing is true and correct.

Executed on (38) JANUARY 31, 2003 at (39) GLENDALE , CA.

(41) _Mabel Jones_

> Residing at (42) 555 MAIN ST.,
>
> EAGLE ROCK, CA

(43) _Ralph Jones_

> Residing at (44) 555 MAIN ST.
>
> EAGLE ROCK, CA

LAST WILL AND TESTAMENT

I, (1) ROBERT SMITH , a resident of (2) LOS ANGELES County, California, being of sound and disposing mind and memory and not acting under duress, menace, fraud or undue influence of any person whomsoever, do make, publish and declare this to be my Last Will and Testament, and I hereby expressly revoke all other wills codicils, and testamentary writings heretofore made by me.

FIRST. I declare that I am (3) DIVORCED . My spouse's name was (4) MARTHA SMITH . I have the following children:

(5) ANDREW SMITH, BORN 10/03/70; AND,

ALISON SMITH, BORN 5/18/72

I have a deceased child who left the following issue now surviving:

(6) NOT APPLICABLE

I have no other children and (7)NOT APPLICABLE deceased children who left issue now surviving.

SECOND. I devise the following personal, tangible property to the follow persons:

(8) 1911 SILVER DOLLAR TO ANDREW SMITH

I devise to (9) ANDREW SMITH AND ALISON SMITH all of my remaining personal effects, household furniture and furnishings, trailers, boats, pictures, works of art and art objects, collections, jewelry, silverware, wearing apparel, collections, sporting goods, and all other articles of household or personal use or ornament at whatsoever time acquired by me and wheresoever situated.

I devise to the following persons the cash amount listed after their respective names:

(10) NOT APPLICABLE

I devise to the following persons the real property described after their respective names. (12) Said real property is given free of all encumbrances or liens thereon.

(11) NOT APPLICABLE

I devise to (13) TERRY HOPP a life estate in the following property located at:(14) 213 CLUB DR., LONG BEACH. After the death of (13) TERRY HOPP said property shall go, outright, to (15) ANDREW SMITH AND ALISON SMITH as the remainder person(s).

I devise all of the rest, residue and remainder of my estate, real, personal and mixed, of whatsoever kind or character and wheresoever situated, of which I die possessed or to which I may in any manner be entitled, to the following persons or entities (16) in the proportions listed after their names (17) in equal shares.

(18) ANDREW SMITH AND ALISON SMITH

In the event any of the above named persons should predecease me or fail to survive me then his or her share shall lapse unless I have specifically named a person to take said bequest in the event of the first beneficiary's death.

Any beneficiary above who fails to survive me by thirty days shall be deemed to have predeceased me.

THIRD: I have intentionally and with full knowledge omitted to provide for my issue, ancestors, relatives and heirs living at the time of my demise, except for such provisions as are made specifically herein.

If any person who is or claims under or through a beneficiary of this Will, or if any person who would be entitled to share in my estate if I died intestate, should in any manner whatsoever, directly or indirectly, attack, contest or seek to impair or invalidate in court any provision of the following:

A. This Will or any Codicil to this Will;

B. Any revocable or irrevocable Trust established by me;

C. Any beneficiary designation executed by me with respect to any insurance policy, any "totten trust" account, any joint tenancy, any "transfer on death" account or any pension plan, or conspire or cooperate with anyone attempting to do any of the actions or things aforesaid, then I hereby specifically disinherit each such person and any devise, share or interest in my estate otherwise given to each such person under this Will or to which each such person might be entitled by law, is hereby revoked and shall pass and be distributed as though each such person had predeceased me leaving no issue or heirs whatsoever.

Any and every individual who asserts, or conspires or cooperates with any person who asserts, any claim against my Estate based on:

D. "Quantum meruit" theory;

E. Common law marriage, Marvin v. Marvin, 18 Cal. 3d 660 (1976) type of agreement or similar theory;

F. Constructive trust theory; or,

G. Oral agreement or written agreement which is to be proved by parole evidence, claiming that I agreed to gift or devise anything to such person or to pay such person or another for services rendered, regardless of whether a court may find that such agreement existed, then I hereby specifically disinherit each such person and any devise, share or interest in my estate otherwise given to each such person under this Will or to which each such person might be entitled by law, is hereby revoked and shall pass and be distributed as though each such person had predeceased me leaving no issue or heirs whatsoever.

FOURTH: I nominate and appoint (34) <u>ANDREW   SMITH</u>   as (35) <u> Executor </u> hereunder (36) without bond. In the event he/she/they should decline, become unable or, for any reason, cease to serve as Executor then I nominate and appoint (37) <u>ALISON SMITH</u> as Executor hereunder (36) without bond.

I authorize my Executor to sell, at either public or private sale, encumber or lease any property belonging to my estate, either with or without public notice, subject to such confirmation as may be required by law, and to hold, manage and operate any such property.

FIFTH. All typed and handwritten "fill-ins" where directed above were made before the execution of this Will and are not initialed by me. All crossed through words and inter-lineations were made before the execution of this Will and are initialed by me.

Except as provided otherwise herein, the masculine, feminine, and neuter gender and the singular or plural number, shall each be deemed to include the others whenever the context so indicates.

IN WITNESS WHEREOF, I have hereunto set my hand this

(38) <u>JANUARY 31, 2003</u> at (39) <u>GLENDALE</u>, CA.

(40) <u>*Robert Smith*</u>

The foregoing instrument, consisting of five pages, including the page on which this attestation clause is completed and signed, was at the date hereof by (1) <u>ROBERT SMITH</u> signed as and declared to be his/her Will, in the presence of us who, at his/her request and in his/her presence, and in the presence of each other, have subscribed our names as witnesses thereto. Each of us observed the signing of this Will by (1) <u>ROBERT SMITH</u> and by each other subscribing witness and knows that each signature is the true signature of the person whose name was signed.

Each of us is now an adult and a competent witness and resides at the address set forth after his or her name.

We are acquainted with (1) ROBERT SMITH . At this time, he/she is over the age of eighteen years, and to the best of our knowledge, he/she is of sound mind and is not acting under

duress, menace, fraud, misrepresentation, or undue influence.

We declare under penalty of perjury that the foregoing is true and correct.

Executed on (38) JANUARY 31, 2003 at (39) GLENDALE , CA.

(41) *Mabel Jones*

                  Residing at (42) 555 MAIN ST.,

                   EAGLE ROCK, CA

(43) *Ralph Jones*

                  Residing at (44) 555 MAIN ST.

                   EAGLE ROCK, CA

APPENDIX D
BLANK FORMS

Choosing the correct form is very important. The NOMINATION OF GUARDIAN, forms 1 and 2, give you two selections. Form 1 should be used when you are concerned about the acceptance of others over your choice of the guardian of the person and/or the estate of your minor children. Form 2 should be used when it is unlikely there will be a controversy over your choice. If you are nominating one person as the guardian of the person of your minor children and another person as the guardian of the estate of your minor children, you may use form 1 for one nomination and form 2 for another.

The will forms are divided into four categories. You should first determine which category you are in and then pick only from the forms within that category. Forms 3 through form 9 are designed for persons who are married and have children. Forms 10 through form 12 are designed for persons who are married and have no children. Forms 13 through form 17 are designed for persons who are unmarried and have children, and forms 18 through form 20 are designed for persons who are unmarried and have no children.

Table of Forms

form 1: Nomination of Guardian—*Use this form when you do not anticipate any conflict over your nomination.*

form 2: Nomination of Guardian—*Use this form when you suspect there may be a conflict over the appointment of the guardian.*

form 3: Last Will and Testament—All to spouse, then all to adult children (simple). *Use this form if you want all of your estate to pass outright to your spouse or outright to your adult children if your spouse fails to survive you.*

form 4: Last Will and Testament—All to spouse, then to children in custodianship. *Use this form if you want all of your estate to pass to your spouse. If your spouse does not survive you, then to your children, in equal shares, at least one of whom is under the age of 25. For any children under the age you select (you must select between ages 18 and 25) his or her share is held by a custodian under the Uniform Transfers to Minors Act. If your estate is relatively modest, you expect that your estate would be liquidated if you die after your spouse and you do not mind if each of your children receives his or her share of the estate by age 25 then this may be the proper form for you.*

form 5: Last Will and Testament—All to spouse, then all to children, in trust for children. *Use this form if you want all of your estate to pass to your spouse. If your spouse does not survive you, then your estate goes into trust for your children, in equal shares. You select the age(s) for distribution of the principal of each child's share of the trust to that child. If your estate is larger or you wish to delay the distribution of a child's inheritance beyond age 25, then this form may be more appropriate for you than form 4.*

form 6: Last Will and Testament—Spouse, with gifts to children and/or others, simple disposition. *Use this form if you want your estate to pass outright to your spouse and your children and/or others.*

form 7: Last Will and Testament—Spouse, children, and/or others create life estate. *Use this form if you want part of your estate to pass outright to your spouse, your children, and/or others and you want to create a life estate in a certain property. Most likely use of this form would be if you wanted to leave a life estate in real estate (i.e., your residence) to your spouse, with the property then passing outright to your children at the death of your spouse. The life estate bequest in the property would make it impossible for the life tenant (i.e., your spouse) to leave the property to someone other than the persons you name as the remaindermen (i.e., your children).*

form 8: Last Will and Testament—Spouse, children, and/or others with trust for one or more persons. *Use this form if you want a portion of your estate to pass outright to your spouse, and/or your children, and/or others, and you want a part of your estate to pass to your spouse and/or your children and/or others in trust wherein you make decisions regarding the distribution of the trust to either the named beneficiary upon reaching certain ages (first option starting at 3.a. or to another beneficiary, outright, upon the death of the first trust beneficiary (second option starting at 3.a.). If you use this form, be certain to cross through the section 3.a. you are NOT using. (Remember that the second option starting at 3.a. has two options as to 3.b. and you must cross through the section 3.b. you do not select.) This form would be used when you want a portion of your estate to be held in trust for the benefit of a beneficiary. If you want a portion of your estate held in trust for your spouse form 9 is likely a better choice. (This trust does not qualify for the marital deduction benefit.)*

form 9: Last Will and Testament—Spouse, children, and/or others, trust for apouse, remainder to children or others. *Use this form if you want a portion of your estate to pass outright to your* *spouse, and/or your children, and/or others, and you want a part of your estate to be held in trust for the benefit of your spouse's lifetime with the trust estate being distributed at the death of your spouse to the person(s) you designate. (This trust does qualify for the marital deduction.)*

form 10: Last Will and Testament—Spouse, no children, then all to others. *Use this form if you want all of your estate to pass outright to your spouse or outright to the beneficiaries you name if your spouse fails to survive you.*

form 11: Last Will and Testament—Spouse and/or others with trust for spouse and remainder to others (no children). *Use this form if you want a portion of your estate to pass outright to your spouse, and/or others, and you want a part of your estate to pass to your spouse, in trust, for his or her lifetime and then be distributed, outright, to the persons you designate upon the death of your spouse.*

form 12: Last Will and Testament—Spouse and/or others (simple), no children. *Use this form if you want your estate to pass outright to your spouse and/or others.*

form 13: Last Will and Testament—No spouse, all to children, and/or others (simple). *Use this form if you want your estate to pass outright to your children and/or others.*

form 14: Last Will and Testament—No spouse, all to children in custodianship. *Use this form if you have at least one child under the age of 25 years and you want all of your estate to pass to a custodian under the Uniform Transfers to Minors Act for the benefit of your children, in equal shares. For any children under the age you select (you must select between ages 18 and 25), his or her share is held, managed, and distributed by the custodian you select. If your estate is relatively modest, and you expect that your estate would be liquidated if you die after your spouse and you do not mind if each of your children receives his or her share of the estate by age 25 then this may be the proper form for you.*

form 15: Last Will and Testament—No spouse, to children and/or others, create a life estate for someone. *Use this form if you want a portion of your estate to pass outright to your children and/or others and you want a part of your estate to pass to someone for his or her lifetime. It would then be distributed, outright, to the persons you designate upon the death of the life tenant. This form would most likely be used when your children are adults and the life tenant is a relative who needs the use or income from the property selected for the life tenancy, but whom you are either worried would lose the property or upon the death of the life tenant, would leave the property to someone other than whom you would like to see receive it.*

form 16: Last Will and Testament—No spouse, to children and/or others with trust for minors/adults. *Use this form if you want all of your estate to go into trust for your children, in equal shares. You select the age(s) for distribution of the principal of each child's share of the trust. If your estate is larger or you wish to delay the distribution of a child's inheritance beyond age 25, then this form may be more appropriate for you than form 14.*

form 17: Last Will and Testament—No spouse, no children, all to others with trust. *Use this form if you want a portion of your estate to pass outright to others and you want a part of your estate to pass to others in trust wherein you make decisions regarding the distribution of the trust to either the named beneficiary upon reaching certain ages (first option starting at 3.a. or to another beneficiary, outright, upon the death of the first trust beneficiary, second option starting at 3.a. If you use this form be certain to cross through the section 3.a. you are NOT using (remember that the second option starting at 3.a. has two options as to 3.b. and you must cross through the section 3.b. you do not select). This form would be used when you want a portion of your estate to be held in trust for the benefit of a beneficiary who is unable to manage assets.*

form 18: Simple Will—No spouse, no children, all to others (simple). *Use this form if you want your estate to pass outright to the persons you designate.*

form 19: Last Will and Testament—No spouse, no children, to others and create a life estate. *Use this form if you want a portion of your estate to pass outright to the persons you designate and want a part of your estate to pass to someone for his or her lifetime and then be distributed, outright, to the persons you designate upon the death of the life tenant.*

form 20: Last Will and Testament—No spouse, no children, with trust for one or more persons. *Use this form if you want a portion of your estate to pass outright to the persons you designate and a part of your estate to pass to the person(s) you designate in trust wherein you make decisions regarding the distribution of the trust to either the named beneficiary upon reaching certain ages (first option starting at 3.a. or to another beneficiary, outright, upon the death of the first trust beneficiary (second option starting at 3.a.). If you use this form, be certain to cross through the section 3.a. you are NOT using (remember that the second option starting at 3.a. has two options as to 3.b. and you must cross through the section 3.b. you do not select). This form would be used when you want a portion of your estate to be held in trust for the benefit of a beneficiary most likely because they are unable to manage assets.*

form 21: Codicil to Last Will and Testament—*This form can be used to change one section of your will.*

Nomination of Guardian

I (1)_____, resident of (2)_____ County, California, declare as follows:

1. I am the parent of (5)

2. In the event I am deceased I wish that (45)_____ be appointed as guardian of the person and estate of each of my minor children, to serve without bond. I understand that said nominated guardian may live in another State at the time of his/her appointment. I expressly consent to the removal of my children to said State if it will facilitate his guardianship appointment;

3. I further instruct my Trustee/Executor to permit (45)_____ to reside in my home during the pendency of his appointment as guardian for a period not to exceed 90 days. I further instruct that any reasonable expenses they may incur in his quest to be appointed guardian whether or not he is actually appointed guardian;

The appointment of (45)_____ is extremely important to me as said nominated guardian shares the same philosophy of child raising as do I and the placement of my children in his care would result in the least trauma to their life.

4. In the event he declines or is unable, for any reason, to so act, I then appoint (46)_____ as said guardian the age of majority at the time of my death to serve without bond.

5. I further permit the guardian of our children to use the estates of my children in the compliance of our request that our children have liberal and appropriate visitation with their family.

Executed on (38)_____, at (39)_____, California.

_____

(40)

_____

(41) Witness

This page intentionally left blank.

Nomination of Guardian

I (1)_____, resident of (2)_____ County, California, declare as follows:

1. I am the parent of (5)

2. In the event I am deceased I wish that (45)_____ be appointed as guardian of the person and estate of my minor children, to serve without bond.

3. In the event he declines or is unable, for any reason, to so act, I then appoint (46)_____ _____ as said guardian the age of majority at the time of my deathto serve without bond.

Executed on (38)_____, at (39)_____, California.

_____

(40)

_____

(41) Witness

This page intentionally left blank.

Last Will and Testament

I, (1)_____, a resident of (2)_____ County, California, being of sound and disposing mind and memory and not acting under duress, menace, fraud or undue influence of any person whomsoever, do make, publish and declare this to be my Last Will and Testament, and I hereby expressly revoke all other wills, codicils, and testamentary writings heretofore made by me.

FIRST. I declare that I am married. My spouse's name is (3)_____. I have the following children:

(5)

I have a deceased child who left the following issue now surviving:

(6)

I have no other children and (7)_____ deceased children who left issue now surviving.

SECOND. I devise all of estate to my spouse. In the event my spouse should predecease me then I devise all my aforesaid estate to the Custodian under the Uniform Gift to Minors Act hereinafter named, to have and to hold upon the purposes and conditions of said act. I am secure in the knowledge that said Custodian will retain those items of personal use or sentimental value for my child or children in a manner I have made known or will make known to said Custodian.

My Executor, in making distribution to the Custodian, shall allocate the estate properties into as many shares as I have children then living and children then deceased who left issue then living. One such equal share shall be set aside for each of my children then living and one such equal share shall be set aside for the issue then living, by right of representation, of each of my children who are then deceased but left issue then living.

The Custodian may deposit any portion of a child's share in an IRC 529 college savings plan for the benefit of said child.

Upon each minor attaining the age of (29) _____ years, the Custodian shall deliver to said child all of the remainder of his or her share.

In the event a child should die before distribution to him or her of his or her share, his or her share on hand at the time of his death shall thereupon be apportioned and distributed to his or her surviving issue, by right of representation. If such child should die before complete distribution to him or her of his or her share and leave no surviving issue, then the balance of the share then on hand shall go and be distributed to my heirs to be determined according to the laws of the State of California then in effect relating to the intestate succession of separate property not acquired from a predeceased spouse.

Each beneficiary hereunder is hereby prohibited from anticipating, encumbering, assigning, or in any other manner alienating his or her interest in either income or principal, and is without power so to do, nor shall such interest be subject to his or her liabilities or obligations, nor to attachment, execution, or other legal processes, bankruptcy proceedings or claims of creditors or others. The Trustee may, however, deposit in any bank designated in writing by a beneficiary, to his or her credit, income or principal payable to such beneficiary.

I nominate and appoint (30)_____ as Custodian hereunder (32) without bond. In the event he/she or both of them should decline to act, or for any other reason, be unable to act as Custodian then I appoint (33) _____ as Custodian hereunder (32) without bond.

THIRD: I have intentionally and with full knowledge omitted to provide for my issue, ancestors, relatives and heirs living at the time of my demise, except for such provisions as are made specifically herein.

If any person who is or claims under or through a beneficiary of this Will, or if any person who would be entitled to share in my estate if I died intestate, should in any manner whatsoever, directly or indirectly, attack, contest or seek to impair or invalidate in court any provision of the following:

A. This Will or any Codicil to this Will;

B. Any revocable or irrevocable Trust established by me;

C. Any beneficiary designation executed by me with respect to any insurance policy, any "totten trust" account, any joint tenancy, any "transfer on death" account or any pension plan, or conspire or cooperate with anyone attempting to do any of the actions or things aforesaid, then I hereby specifically disinherit each such person and any devise, share or interest in my estate otherwise given to each such person under this Will or to which each such person might be entitled by law, is hereby revoked and shall pass and be distributed as though each such person had predeceased me leaving no issue or heirs whatsoever.

Any and every individual who asserts, or conspires or cooperates with any person who asserts, any claim against my Estate based on:

D. "Quantum meruit" theory;

E. Common law marriage, Marvin v. Marvin, 18 Cal. 3d 660 (1976) type of agreement or similar theory;

F. Constructive trust theory; or,

G. Oral agreement or written agreement which is to be proved by parole evidence, claiming that I agreed to gift or devise anything to such person or to pay such person or another for services rendered, regardless of whether a court may find that such agreement existed, then I hereby specifically disinherit each such person and any devise, share or interest in my estate otherwise given to each such person under this Will or to which each such person might be entitled by law, is hereby revoked and shall pass and be distributed as though each such person had predeceased me leaving no issue or heirs whatsoever.

FOURTH: I nominate and appoint my spouse as Executor hereunder without bond. In the event my spouse should decline, become unable or, for any reason, cease to serve as Executor then I nominate and appoint (37) _____ as Executor hereunder (36) without bond.

I authorize my Executor to sell, at either public or private sale, encumber or lease any property belonging to my estate, either with or without public notice, subject to such confirmation as may be required by law, and to hold, manage and operate any such property.

FIFTH. All typed and handwritten "fill-ins" where directed above were made before the execution of this Will and are not initialed by me. All crossed through words and inter-lineations were made before the execution of this Will and are initialed by me.

The masculine, feminine, and neuter gender and the singular or plural number, shall each be deemed to include the others whenever the context so indicates.

IN WITNESS WHEREOF, I have hereunto set my hand this (38)_____ at (39) _____, CA.

(40)_____

The foregoing instrument, consisting of four pages, including the page on which this attestation clause is completed and signed, was at the date hereof by (1)_____ signed as and declared to be his/her Will, in the presence of us who, at his/her request and in his/her presence, and in the presence of each other, have subscribed our names as witnesses thereto. Each of us observed the signing of this Will by (1)_____ and by each other subscribing witness and knows that each signature is the true signature of the person whose name was signed.

Each of us is now an adult and a competent witness and resides at the address set forth after his or her name.

We are acquainted with (1)_____. At this time, he/she is over the age of eighteen years, and to the best of our knowledge, he/she is of sound mind and is not acting under duress, menace, fraud, misrepresentation, or undue influence.

We declare under penalty of perjury that the foregoing is true and correct.

Executed on (38)_____ at (39)_____, CA.

(41)_____ Residing at (42) _____

_____

(43)_____ Residing at (44) _____

_____

Last Will and Testament

I, (1)_____, a resident of (2)_____ County, California, being of sound and disposing mind and memory and not acting under duress, menace, fraud or undue influence of any person whomsoever, do make, publish and declare this to be my Last Will and Testament, and I hereby expressly revoke all other wills, codicils, and testamentary writings heretofore made by me.

FIRST. I declare that I am married. My spouse's name is (4)_____.
I have the following children:

(5)

I have a deceased child who left the following issue now surviving:

(6)

I have no other children and (7)_____ deceased children who left issue now surviving.

SECOND. I devise all of estate to my spouse. In the event my spouse should predecease me then I devise all my aforesaid estate to the Trustee hereinafter named, to have and to hold upon the uses, trusts, purposes and conditions hereinafter provided. I am secure in the knowledge that my Trustee will retain those items of personal use or sentimental value for my child or children in a manner I have made known or will make known to my Trustee.

My Executor, in making distribution to the Trustee, shall allocate the trust properties into as many shares as I have children then living and children then deceased who left issue then living. One such equal share shall be set aside for each of my children then living and one such equal share shall be set aside for the issue then living, by right of representation, of each of my children who are then deceased but left issue then living. Said shares shall be held, administered, and distributed as provided in the following sections:

Each share set aside for a child of mine shall be held, administered and delivered for and to such beneficiary as follows:

1. The net income from the trust while said beneficiary is under 19 years of age and not a high school graduate shall be added to principal, from which the Trustee shall pay to or for the benefit of such beneficiary such sums as in the Trustee's discretion the Trustee shall deem necessary for such beneficiary's proper care, comfort, maintenance, support or education.

In making payments for the benefit of any beneficiary pursuant to this section 1, the Trustee shall construe his authority liberally to permit payments reasonably necessary to ease the financial burden on the guardian of the person of such beneficiary or other suitable individual with whom they reside, and on his family, resulting from such beneficiary's presence in his household.

2. Upon the beneficiary reaching 19 years of age or finishing high school(whichever occurs first), the Trustee shall pay to or apply for his or her benefit, from his or her trust, as much of the trust principal as the Trustee, in the Trustee's discretion, considers appropriate pursuant to sections 3 and 4 following.

3. After the beneficiary attains 19 years of age or finishes high school (whichever occurs first), the Trustee may, in the Trustee's discretion, pay to or apply from her trust, such amounts necessary for her education. For purposes hereof, education shall mean enrollment, attendance, and satisfactory progression towards a degree as a student at a recognized and accredited college, university, or similar institution of higher learning, including any graduate, professional school or college or trade school. Such educational payments and benefits shall include tuition, books, all direct educational costs and fees, and all reasonable living and transportation expenses. Payments hereunder shall be made during vacation periods within the regular school term under which the beneficiary is attending school and during "summer vacation" or similar vacation period between the regular school terms.

The Trustee may invest any portion of a beneficiary's trust share in an IRC 529 college savings plan for the benefit of said beneficiary.

4. If the beneficiary, his or her spouse, or any of his children should at any time or from time to time be in need, in the discretion of the Trustee, of funds due to illness, infirmity or other physical or mental disability or any emergency, the Trustee may relieve or contribute toward the relief of any such need or needs of the beneficiary by paying to him or her or using and applying for his or her benefit, such sum or sums out of the income and/or principal of his or her trust as the Trustee, in the Trustee's discretion, may deem necessary or advisable.

5. Upon the beneficiary attaining the age of 21 years, the Trustee shall begin to pay the beneficiary all of the net income, in monthly or other convenient installments, from the trust.

6. Upon the beneficiary attaining the age of (21)_____ years, the Trustee shall distribute and deliver to such beneficiary one-half of his trust estate. Upon each beneficiary attaining the age of (22)_____ years, the Trustee shall distribute and deliver to such beneficiary all of the remainder of his or her trust estate.

7. If, upon the attaining of the above ages, the Trustee suspects that said beneficiary may be abusing drugs, the Trustee may require the beneficiary to take a reasonable drug test. If the beneficiary fails said drug test, the Trustee shall defer said principal payment to the

beneficiary until the beneficiary passes said drug test. After a failed drug test, subsequent drug tests shall be administered at six month intervals. In the event a beneficiary fails a drug test, the Trustee may use said beneficiary's trust estate to pay for a drug abuse rehabilitation program and may require the beneficiary to enroll and to complete said program as a condition precedent to the taking of a subsequent drug test.

8. In the event the beneficiary should die before complete distribution to him or her of his or her trust estate, his or her entire trust estate on hand at the time of his death shall thereupon be apportioned and distributed to his or her surviving issue, by right of representation. If such beneficiary should die before complete distribution to him or her of his or her trust estate and leave no surviving issue, then the balance of the trust estate then on hand shall go and be distributed to my heirs to be determined according to the laws of the State of California then in effect relating to the intestate succession of separate property not acquired from a predeceased spouse.

9. Each beneficiary hereunder is hereby prohibited from anticipating, encumbering, assigning, or in any other manner alienating his or her interest in either income or principal, and is without power so to do, nor shall such interest be subject to his or her liabilities or obligations, nor to attachment, execution, or other legal processes, bankruptcy proceedings or claims of creditors or others. The Trustee may, however, deposit in any bank designated in writing by a beneficiary, to his or her credit, income or principal payable to such beneficiary.

10. If, at any time, a trust created hereunder shall, in the sole judgment of the Trustee, be of the aggregate principal value of Fifty Thousand Dollars ($50,000.00) or less, the Trustee may, but need not, terminate such trust and distribute the assets thereof in the Trustee's possession to the beneficiary or beneficiaries, at the time of the current income thereof, and if there is more than one beneficiary, in the proportion in which they are beneficiaries.

11. I nominate and appoint (25)_____ as (26)_____ Trustee hereunder (27) without bond. If he/she/both of them should die, resign, decline to act, or for any other reason, is unable to act as Trustee then I appoint (28) _____
as Trustee hereunder (27) without bond.

THIRD: I have intentionally and with full knowledge omitted to provide for my issue, ancestors, relatives and heirs living at the time of my demise, except for such provisions as are made specifically herein.

If any person who is or claims under or through a beneficiary of this Will, or if any person who would be entitled to share in my estate if I died intestate, should in any manner whatsoever, directly or indirectly, attack, contest or seek to impair or invalidate in court any provision of the following:

A. This Will or any Codicil to this Will;

B. Any revocable or irrevocable Trust established by me;

C. Any beneficiary designation executed by me with respect to any insurance policy, any "totten trust" account, any joint tenancy, any "transfer on death" account or any pension plan, or conspire or cooperate with anyone attempting to do any of the actions or things aforesaid, then I hereby specifically disinherit each such person and any devise, share or interest in my estate otherwise given to each such person under this Will or to which each such person might be entitled by law, is hereby revoked and shall pass and be distributed as though each such person had predeceased me leaving no issue or heirs whatsoever.

Any and every individual who asserts, or conspires or cooperates with any person who asserts, any claim against my Estate based on:

D. "Quantum meruit" theory;

E. Common law marriage, Marvin v. Marvin, 18 Cal. 3d 660 (1976) type of agreement or similar theory;

F. Constructive trust theory; or,

G. Oral agreement or written agreement which is to be proved by parole evidence, claiming that I agreed to gift or devise anything to such person or to pay such person or another for services rendered, regardless of whether a court may find that such agreement existed, then I hereby specifically disinherit each such person and any devise, share or interest in my estate otherwise given to each such person under this Will or to which each such person might be entitled by law, is hereby revoked and shall pass and be distributed as though each such person had predeceased me leaving no issue or heirs whatsoever.

FOURTH: I nominate and appoint my spouse as Executor hereunder without bond. In the event he should decline, become unable or, for any reason, cease to serve as Executor then I nominate and appoint (34) _____ as (35)_____ Executor hereunder (36) without bond.

I authorize my Executor to sell, at either public or private sale, encumber or lease any property belonging to my estate, either with or without public notice, subject to such confirmation as may be required by law, and to hold, manage and operate any such property.

FIFTH: All typed and handwritten "fill-ins" where directed above were made before the execution of this Will and are not initialed by me. All crossed through words and inter-lineations were made before the execution of this Will and are initialed by me.

Except as provided otherwise herein, the masculine, feminine, and neuter gender and the singular or plural number, shall each be deemed to include the others whenever the context so indicates.

IN WITNESS WHEREOF, I have hereunto set my hand this

(38)_____ at (39) _____, CA.

(40)_____

The foregoing instrument, consisting of five pages, including the page on which this attestation clause is completed and signed, was at the date hereof by (1)_____ signed as and declared to be his/her Will, in the presence of us who, at his/her request and in his/her presence, and in the presence of each other, have subscribed our names as witnesses thereto. Each of us observed the signing of this Will by (1)_____ and by each other subscribing witness and knows that each signature is the true signature of the person whose name was signed.

Each of us is now an adult and a competent witness and resides at the address set forth after his or her name.

We are acquainted with (1)_____. At this time, he/she is over the age of eighteen years, and to the best of our knowledge, he/she is of sound mind and is not acting under duress, menace, fraud, misrepresentation, or undue influence.

We declare under penalty of perjury that the foregoing is true and correct.

Executed on (38)_____ at (39)_____, CA.

(41)_____Residing at (42)_____

_____

(43)_____Residing at (44)_____

_____

This page intentionally left blank.

Last Will and Testament

I, (1)_____, a resident of (2)_____ County, California, being of sound and disposing mind and memory and not acting under duress, menace, fraud or undue influence of any person whomsoever, do make, publish and declare this to be my Last Will and Testament, and I hereby expressly revoke all other wills, codicils, and testamentary writings heretofore made by me.

FIRST. I declare that I am married. My spouse's name is (4)_____. I have the following children:

(5)

I have a deceased child who left the following issue now surviving:

(6)

I have no other children and (7)_____ deceased children who left issue now surviving.

SECOND. I devise the following personal, tangible property:

(8)

I devise to (9)_____ all of my remaining personal effects, household furniture and furnishings, trailers, boats, pictures, works of art and art objects, collections, jewelry, silverware, wearing apparel, collections, sporting goods, and all other articles of household or personal use or ornament at whatsoever time acquired by me and wheresoever situated.

I devise to the following persons the cash amount listed after their respective names:

(10)

I devise to the following persons the real property described after their respective names. (12) Said real property is given free of all encumbrances or liens thereon.

(11)

I devise all of the rest, residue and remainder of my estate, real, personal and mixed, of whatsoever kind or character and wheresoever situated, of which I die possessed or to which I may in any manner be entitled, to the following persons or entities (16) in the proportions listed after their names (17) in equal shares.

(18)

In the event any of the above named persons should predecease me or fail to survive me then his or her share shall lapse unless I have specifically named a person to take said bequest in the event of the first beneficiary's death.

Any beneficiary above who fails to survive me by thirty days shall be deemed to have predeceased me.

THIRD: I have intentionally and with full knowledge omitted to provide for my issue, ancestors, relatives and heirs living at the time of my demise, except for such provisions as are made specifically herein.

If any person who is or claims under or through a beneficiary of this Will, or if any person who would be entitled to share in my estate if I died intestate, should in any manner whatsoever, directly or indirectly, attack, contest or seek to impair or invalidate in court any provision of the following:

A. This Will or any Codicil to this Will;

B. Any revocable or irrevocable Trust established by me;

C. Any beneficiary designation executed by me with respect to any insurance policy, any "totten trust" account, any joint tenancy, any "transfer on death" account or any pension plan, or conspire or cooperate with anyone attempting to do any of the actions or things aforesaid, then I hereby specifically disinherit each such person and any devise, share or interest in my estate otherwise given to each such person under this Will or to which each such person might be entitled by law, is hereby revoked and shall pass and be distributed as though each such person had predeceased me leaving no issue or heirs whatsoever.

Any and every individual who asserts, or conspires or cooperates with any person who asserts, any claim against my Estate based on:

D. "Quantum meruit" theory;

E. Common law marriage, Marvin v. Marvin, 18 Cal. 3d 660 (1976) type of agreement or similar theory;

F. Constructive trust theory; or,

G. Oral agreement or written agreement which is to be proved by parole evidence, claiming that I agreed to gift or devise anything to such person or to pay such person or another for services rendered, regardless of whether a court may find that such agreement existed, then I hereby specifically disinherit each such person and any devise, share or interest in my estate otherwise given to each such person under this Will or to which each such person might be entitled by law, is hereby revoked and shall pass and be distributed as though each such person had predeceased me leaving no issue or heirs whatsoever.

FOURTH: I nominate and appoint (34) _____ as (35) _____ Executor hereunder (36) without bond. In the event he/she/they should decline, become unable or, for any reason, cease to serve as Executor then I nominate and appoint (37) _____ as Executor hereunder (36) without bond.

I authorize my Executor to sell, at either public or private sale, encumber or lease any property belonging to my estate, either with or without public notice, subject to such confirmation as may be required by law, and to hold, manage and operate any such property.

FIFTH. All typed or handwritten "fill-ins" where directed above were made before the execution of this Will and are not initialed by me. All cross through words and inter-lineations were made before the execution of this Will and are initialed by me.

Except as provided otherwise herein, the masculine, feminine, and neuter gender and the singular or plural number, shall each be deemed to include the others whenever the context so indicates.

IN WITNESS WHEREOF, I have hereunto set my hand this (38)_____ at (39) _____, CA.

(40)_____

The foregoing instrument, consisting of four pages, including the page on which this attestation clause is completed and signed, was at the date hereof by (1)_____ signed as and declared to be his/her Will, in the presence of us who, at his/her request and in his/her presence, and in the presence of each other, have subscribed our names as witnesses thereto. Each of us observed the signing of this Will by (1)_____ and by each other subscribing witness and knows that each signature is the true signature of the person whose name was signed.

Each of us is now an adult and a competent witness and resides at the address set forth after his or her name.

We are acquainted with (1)_____. At this time, he/she is over the age of eighteen years, and to the best of our knowledge, he/she is of sound mind and is not acting under duress, menace, fraud, misrepresentation, or undue influence.

We declare under penalty of perjury that the foregoing is true and correct.

Executed on (38)_____ at (39)_____, CA.

(41)_____Residing at (42)_____

_____

(43)_____ Residing at (44)_____

_____

Last Will and Testament

I, (1)_____, a resident of (2)_____ County, California, being of sound and disposing mind and memory and not acting under duress, menace, fraud or undue influence of any person whomsoever, do make, publish and declare this to be my Last Will and Testament, and I hereby expressly revoke all other wills, codicils, and testamentary writings heretofore made by me.

FIRST. I declare that I am married. My spouse's name is (4)_____. I have the following children:

(5)

I have a deceased child who left the following issue now surviving:

(6)

I have no other children and (7)_____ deceased children who left issue now surviving.

SECOND. I devise the following personal, tangible property:

(8)

I devise to (9)_____ all of my remaining personal effects, household furniture and furnishings, trailers, boats, pictures, works of art and art objects, collections, jewelry, silverware, wearing apparel, collections, sporting goods, and all other articles of household or personal use or ornament at whatsoever time acquired by me and wheresoever situated.

I devise to the following persons the cash amount listed after their respective names:

(10)

I devise to the following persons the real property described after their respective names. (12) Said real property is given free of all encumbrances or liens thereon.

(11)

In the event any of the above named persons should predecease me or fail to survive me then his or her share shall lapse unless I have specifically named a person to take said bequest in the event of the first beneficiary's death.

Any beneficiary above who fails to survive me by thirty days shall be deemed to have predeceased me.

I devise all of the rest, residue and remainder of my estate, real, personal and mixed, of whatsoever kind or character and wheresoever situated, of which I die possessed or to which I may in any manner be entitled, to the following persons or entities (16) in the proportions listed after their names (17) in equal shares.

(18)

(19)_____ shares to the Trustee hereinafter named, to have and to hold for the benefit of (20)_____upon the uses, trusts, purposes and conditions hereinafter provided. 1. If the beneficiary, his or her spouse, or any of his children should at any time or from time to time be in need, in the discretion of the Trustee, of funds due to illness, infirmity or other physical or mental disability or any emergency, the Trustee may relieve or contribute toward the relief of any such need or needs of the beneficiary by paying to him or her or using and applying for his or her benefit, such sum or sums out of the income and/or principal of his or her trust as the Trustee, in the Trustee's discretion, may deem necessary or advisable.

2. The Trustee shall pay the beneficiary all of the net income, in monthly or other convenient installments, from the trust.

3.a. (47 - Option 1 Start) Upon the beneficiary attaining the age of (21)_____ years, the Trustee shall distribute and deliver to such beneficiary one-half of his trust estate. Upon each beneficiary attaining the age of (22)_____ years, the Trustee shall distribute and deliver to such beneficiary all of the remainder of his or her trust estate.

3.b. If, upon the attaining of the above ages, the Trustee suspects that said beneficiary may be abusing drugs and/or alcohol, the Trustee may require the beneficiary to take a reasonable drug and/or alcohol test. If the beneficiary fails said test, the trustee shall defer said principal payment to the beneficiary until the beneficiary passes said test. After a failed test, subsequent drug tests shall be administered at the request of the beneficiary but not less than six months after a prior test. In the event a beneficiary fails a drug and/or alcohol test, the Trustee may use said beneficiary's trust estate to pay for a drug and/or alcohol abuse rehabilitation program and may require the beneficiary to enroll and to complete said program as a condition precedent to the taking of a subsequent drug and/or alcohol test.

3.c. In the event the beneficiary should die before complete distribution to him or her of his or her trust estate, his or her entire trust estate on hand at the time of his death shall thereupon be apportioned and distributed to his or her surviving issue, by right of representation. If such beneficiary should die before complete distribution to him or her of his or her trust estate and leave no surviving issue, then the balance of the trust estate then on hand shall go and be distributed to my heirs to be determined according to the laws of the State of California then in effect relating to the intestate succession of separate property not acquired from a predeceased spouse. (47 - Option 1 End)

OR

3.a. (47 - Option 2 Start) In addition to any other payments to the beneficiary hereunder, the Trustee shall, upon the written request of the beneficiary in December of each calendar year, pay to the beneficiary amounts from principal that the beneficiary requests, not exceeding in any single calendar year the greater of the following amounts: $5,000.00 or 5 percent of the value of the principal of the beneficiary's trust estate; determined as of the end of the calendar year. This right of withdrawal is noncumulative, so that if the beneficiary does not withdraw the full amount permitted to be withdrawn during any calendar year, the right to withdraw the remaining amount will lapse at the end of the calendar year.

3.b. On the death of the beneficiary his or her entire trust estate on hand at the time of his death shall thereupon be apportioned and distributed to (23)_____.
If (23)_____ is then deceased then the trust estate then on hand shall go to (24)_____, if he is then living. (47 - Option 2A End)

OR:

the beneficiary's surviving issue, by right of representation. If such beneficiary should die before complete distribution to him or her of his or her trust estate and leave no surviving issue, then the balance of the trust estate then on hand shall go and be distributed to my heirs to be determined according to the laws of the State of California then in effect relating to the intestate succession of separate property not acquired from a predeceased spouse. (47 - Option 2B End)

4. Each beneficiary hereunder is hereby prohibited from anticipating, encumbering, assigning, or in any other manner alienating his or her interest in either income or principal, and is without power so to do, nor shall such interest be subject to his or her liabilities or obligations, nor to attachment, execution, or other legal processes, bankruptcy proceedings or claims of creditors or others. The Trustee may, however, deposit in any bank designated in writing by a beneficiary, to his or her credit, income or principal payable to such beneficiary.

5. If, at any time, a trust created hereunder shall, in the sole judgment of the Trustee, be of the aggregate principal value of Fifty Thousand Dollars ($50,000.00) or less, the Trustee may, but need not, terminate such trust and distribute the assets thereof in the Trustee's possession to the beneficiary or beneficiaries, at the time of the current income thereof, and if there is more than one beneficiary, in the proportion in which they are beneficiaries.

6. I nominate and appoint (25)_____ as (26)_____ Trustee hereunder (27) without bond. In the event he/she or both of them should die, decline to act, or for any other reason, be unable to act as Trustee then I appoint (28) _____ as Trustee hereunder (27) without bond.

THIRD: I have intentionally and with full knowledge omitted to provide for my issue, ancestors, relatives and heirs living at the time of my demise, except for such provisions as are made specifically herein.

If any person who is or claims under or through a beneficiary of this Will, or if any person who would be entitled to share in my estate if I died intestate, should in any manner whatsoever, directly or indirectly, attack, contest or seek to impair or invalidate in court any provision of the following:

A. This Will or any Codicil to this Will;

B. Any revocable or irrevocable Trust established by me;

C. Any beneficiary designation executed by me with respect to any insurance policy, any "totten trust" account, any joint tenancy, any "transfer on death" account or any pension plan, or conspire or cooperate with anyone attempting to do any of the actions or things aforesaid, then I hereby specifically disinherit each such person and any devise, share or interest in my estate otherwise given to each such person under this Will or to which each such person might be entitled by law, is hereby revoked and shall pass and be distributed as though each such person had predeceased me leaving no issue or heirs whatsoever.

Any and every individual who asserts, or conspires or cooperates with any person who asserts, any claim against my Estate based on:

D. "Quantum meruit" theory;

E. Common law marriage, Marvin v. Marvin, 18 Cal. 3d 660 (1976) type of agreement or similar theory;

F. Constructive trust theory; or,

G. Oral agreement or written agreement which is to be proved by parole evidence, claiming that I agreed to gift or devise anything to such person or to pay such person or another for services rendered, regardless of whether a court may find that such agreement existed, then I hereby specifically disinherit each such person and any devise, share or interest in my estate otherwise given to each such person under this Will or to which each such person might be entitled by law, is hereby revoked and shall pass and be distributed as though each such person had predeceased me leaving no issue or heirs whatsoever.

FOURTH: I nominate and appoint (34) _____ as (35)_____ Executor hereunder (36) without bond. In the event he/she or both of them should decline, become unable or, for any reason, cease to serve as Executor then I nominate and appoint (37) _____ as Executor hereunder (36) without bond.

I authorize my Executor to sell, at either public or private sale, encumber or lease any property belonging to my estate, either with or without public notice, subject to such confirmation as may be required by law, and to hold, manage and operate any such property.

FIFTH. All typed and handwritten "fill-ins" where directed above were made before the execution of this Will and are not initialed by me. All crossed through words and inter-lineations were made before the execution of this Will and are initialed by me.

The masculine, feminine, and neuter gender and the singular or plural number, shall each be deemed to include the others whenever the context so indicates.

IN WITNESS WHEREOF, I have hereunto set my hand this (38)_____ at (39) _____, CA.

(40)_____

The foregoing instrument, consisting of five pages, including the page on which this attestation clause is completed and signed, was at the date hereof by (1)_____ signed as and declared to be his/her Will, in the presence of us who, at his/her request and in his/her presence, and in the presence of each other, have subscribed our names as witnesses thereto. Each of us observed the signing of this Will by (1)_____ and by each other subscribing witness and knows that each signature is the true signature of the person whose name was signed.

Each of us is now an adult and a competent witness and resides at the address set forth after his or her name.

We are acquainted with (1)_____. At this time, he/she is over the age of eighteen years, and to the best of our knowledge, he/she is of sound mind and is not acting under duress, menace, fraud, misrepresentation, or undue influence.

We declare under penalty of perjury that the foregoing is true and correct.

Executed on (38)_____at (39)_____, CA.

(41)_____ Residing at (42) _____

_____

(43)_____ Residing at (44) _____

_____

This page intentionally left blank.

Last Will and Testament

I, (1)_____, a resident of (2)_____ County, California, being of sound and disposing mind and memory and not acting under duress, menace, fraud or undue influence of any person whomsoever, do make, publish and declare this to be my Last Will and Testament, and I hereby expressly revoke all other wills, codicils, and testamentary writings heretofore made by me.

FIRST. I declare that I am married. My spouse's name is (4)_____. I have no children and no issue now living of a deceased child.

SECOND. I devise all of my estate, real, personal and mixed, of whatsoever kind or character and wheresoever situated, of which I die possessed or to which I may in any manner be entitled, to my spouse.

If my spouse fails to survive me then I devise the following personal, tangible property to the follow persons:

(8)

I devise to (9)_____ all of my remaining personal effects, household furniture and furnishings, trailers, boats, pictures, works of art and art objects, collections, jewelry, silverware, wearing apparel, collections, sporting goods, and all other articles of household or personal use or ornament at whatsoever time acquired by me and wheresoever situated.

I devise to the following persons the cash amount listed after their respective names:

(10)

I devise to the following persons the real property described after their respective names. (12) Said real property is given free of all encumbrances or liens thereon.

(11)

I devise all of the rest, residue and remainder of my estate, real, personal and mixed, of whatsoever kind or character and wheresoever situated, of which I die possessed or to which I may in any manner be entitled, to (16) in the pro-portions listed after their names (17) in equal shares.

(18)

In the event any of the above named persons should predecease me or fail to survive me then his or her share shall lapse unless I have specifically named a person to take said bequest in the event of the first beneficiary's death.

Any beneficiary above who fails to survive me by thirty days shall be deemed to have predeceased me.

THIRD. I have intentionally and with full knowledge omitted to provide for my issue, ancestors, relatives and heirs living at the time of my demise, except for such provisions as are made specifically herein.

If any person who is or claims under or through a beneficiary of this Will, or if any person who would be entitled to share in my estate if I died intestate, should in any manner whatsoever, directly or indirectly, attack, contest or seek to impair or invalidate in court any provision of the following:

A. This Will or any Codicil to this Will;

B. Any revocable or irrevocable Trust established by me;

C. Any beneficiary designation executed by me with respect to any insurance policy, any "totten trust" account, any joint tenancy, any "transfer on death" account or any pension plan, or conspire or cooperate with anyone attempting to do any of the actions or things aforesaid, then I hereby specifically disinherit each such person and any devise, share or interest in my estate otherwise given to each such person under this Will or to which each such person might be entitled by law, is hereby revoked and shall pass and be distributed as though each such person had predeceased me leaving no issue or heirs whatsoever.

Any and every individual who asserts, or conspires or cooperates with any person who asserts, any claim against my Estate based on:

D. "Quantum meruit" theory;

E. Common law marriage, Marvin v. Marvin, 18 Cal. 3d 660 (1976) type of agreement or similar theory;

F. Constructive trust theory; or,

G. Oral agreement or written agreement which is to be proved by parole evidence, claiming that I agreed to gift or devise anything to such person or to pay such person or another for services rendered, regardless of whether a court may find that such agreement existed, then I hereby specifically disinherit each such person and any devise, share or interest in my estate otherwise given to each such person under this Will or to which each such person might be entitled by law, is hereby revoked and shall pass and be distributed as though each such person had predeceased me leaving no issue or heirs whatsoever.

FOURTH: I nominate and appoint my spouse as Executor hereunder without bond. In the event my spouse should decline, become unable or, for any reason, cease to serve as Executor then I nominate and appoint (37)_____ as (34) _____ Executor hereunder (36) without bond.

I authorize my Executor to sell, at either public or private sale, encumber or lease any property belonging to my estate, either with or without public notice, subject to such confirmation as may be required by law, and to hold, manage and operate any such property.

FIFTH. All typed and handwritten "fill-ins" where directed above were made before the execution of this Will and are not initialed by me. All crossed through words and inter-lineations were made before the execution of this Will and are initialed by me.

Except as provided otherwise herein, the masculine, feminine, and neuter gender and the singular or plural number, shall each be deemed to include the others whenever the context so indicates.

IN WITNESS WHEREOF, I have hereunto set my hand this (38)_____ at (39) _____, CA.

(40)_____

The foregoing instrument, consisting of four pages, including the page on which this attestation clause is completed and signed, was at the date hereof by (1)_____ signed as and declared to be his/her Will, in the presence of us who, at his/her request and in his/her presence, and in the presence of each other, have subscribed our names as witnesses thereto. Each of us observed the signing of this Will by (1)_____ and by each other subscribing witness and knows that each signature is the true signature of the person whose name was signed.

Each of us is now an adult and a competent witness and resides at the address set forth after his or her name.

We are acquainted with (1)_____. At this time, he/she is over the age of eighteen years, and to the best of our knowledge, he/she is of sound mind and is not acting under duress, menace, fraud, misrepresentation, or undue influence.

We declare under penalty of perjury that the foregoing is true and correct.

Executed on (38)_____ at (39)_____, CA.

(41)_____Residing at (42)_____

_____

(43)_____ Residing at (44)_____

_____

Last Will and Testament

I, (1)_____, a resident of (2)_____ County, California, being of sound and disposing mind and memory and not acting under duress, menace, fraud or undue influence of any person whomsoever, do make, publish and declare this to be my Last Will and Testament, and I hereby expressly revoke all other wills, codicils, and testamentary writings heretofore made by me.

FIRST. I declare that I am married. My spouse's name (4)_____.
I have no children and no deceased children who left issue now surviving.

SECOND. I devise the following personal, tangible property:

(8)

I devise to (9) _____ all of my remaining personal effects, household furniture and furnishings, trailers, boats, pictures, works of art and art objects, collections, jewelry, silverware, wearing apparel, collections, sporting goods, and all other articles of household or personal use or ornament at whatsoever time acquired by me and wheresoever situated.

I devise to the following persons the cash amount listed after their respective names:

(10)

I devise to the following persons the real property described after their respective names. (12) Said real property is given free of all encumbrances or liens thereon.

(11)

In the event any of the above named persons should predecease me or fail to survive me then his or her share shall lapse unless I have specifically named a person to take said bequest in the event of the first beneficiary's death.

Any beneficiary above who fails to survive me by thirty days shall be deemed to have predeceased me.

I devise all of the rest, residue and remainder of my estate, real, personal and mixed, of whatsoever kind or character and wheresoever situated, of which I die possessed or to which I may in any manner be entitled, to the following persons or entities (16) in the proportions listed after their names (17) in equal shares.

(18)

(19)_____ shares to the Trustee hereinafter named, to have and to hold for the benefit of my spouse upon the uses, trusts, purposes and conditions hereinafter provided.

1. If my spouse or any of his or her children should at any time or from time to time be in need, in the discretion of the Trustee, of funds due to illness, infirmity or other physical or mental disability or any emergency, the Trustee may relieve or contribute toward the relief of any such need or needs of my spouse by paying to him or her or using and applying for his or her benefit, such sum or sums out of the income and/or principal of his or her trust as the Trustee, in the Trustee's discretion, may deem necessary or advisable.

2. The Trustee shall pay my spouse all of the net income, in monthly or other convenient installments, from the trust.

3. My spouse shall have the right to require the Trustee to convert any non-income producing asset into an income producing asset.

4. Upon the death of my spouse the Trustee shall distribute any accrued but undistributed income to my spouse's estate. The Trustee shall distribute, free of trust, the remaining trust properties to: (23)_____.

5. My spouse is prohibited from anticipating, encumbering, assigning, or in any other manner alienating his or her interest in either income or principal, and is without power so to do, nor shall such interest be subject to his or her liabilities or obligations, nor to attachment, execution, or other legal processes, bankruptcy proceedings or claims of creditors or others. The Trustee may, however, deposit in any bank designated in writing by my spouse, to his or her credit, income or principal payable to my spouse.

6. I nominate and appoint (25)_____ as (26)_____ Trustee hereunder (27) without bond. In the event he/she/they should die, decline to act, or for any other reason, be unable to act as Trustee then I appoint (28) _____ as Trustee hereunder (27) without bond.

THIRD: I have intentionally and with full knowledge omitted to provide for my issue, ancestors, relatives and heirs living at the time of my demise, except for such provisions as are made specifically herein.

If any person who is or claims under or through a beneficiary of this Will, or if any person who would be entitled to share in my estate if I died intestate, should in any manner whatsoever, directly or indirectly, attack, contest or seek to impair or invalidate in court any provision of the following:

A. This Will or any Codicil to this Will;

B. Any revocable or irrevocable Trust established by me;

C. Any beneficiary designation executed by me with respect to any insurance policy, any "totten trust" account, any joint tenancy, any "transfer on death" account or any pension plan, or conspire or cooperate with anyone attempting to do any of the actions or things aforesaid, then I hereby specifically disinherit each such person and any devise, share or interest in my estate otherwise given to each such person under this Will or to which each such person might be entitled by law, is hereby revoked and shall pass and be distributed as though each such person had predeceased me leaving no issue or heirs whatsoever.

Any and every individual who asserts, or conspires or cooperates with any person who asserts, any claim against my Estate based on:

D. "Quantum meruit" theory;

E. Common law marriage, Marvin v. Marvin, 18 Cal. 3d 660 (1976) type of agreement or similar theory;

F. Constructive trust theory; or,

G. Oral agreement or written agreement which is to be proved by parole evidence, claiming that I agreed to gift or devise anything to such person or to pay such person or another for services rendered, regardless of whether a court may find that such agreement existed, then I hereby specifically disinherit each such person and any devise, share or interest in my estate otherwise given to each such person under this Will or to which each such person might be entitled by law, is hereby revoked and shall pass and be distributed as though each such person had predeceased me leaving no issue or heirs whatsoever.

FOURTH: I nominate and appoint (34) _____ as (35)_____ Executor hereunder (36) without bond. In the event he/she/they should decline, become unable or, for any reason, cease to serve as Executor then I nominate and appoint (37) _____ as Executor hereunder (36) without bond.

I authorize my Executor to sell, at either public or private sale, encumber or lease any property belonging to my estate, either with or without public notice, subject to such confirmation as may be required by law, and to hold, manage and operate any such property.

FIFTH. All typed and handwritten "fill-ins" where directed above were made before the execution of this Will and are not initialed by me. All crossed through words and inter-lineations were made before the execution of this Will and are initialed by me.

The masculine, feminine, and neuter gender and the singular or plural number, shall each be deemed to include the others whenever the context so indicates.

IN WITNESS WHEREOF, I have hereunto set my hand this (38)_____ ____ at (39) _____, CA.

(40_____

The foregoing instrument, consisting of four pages, including the page on which this attestation clause is completed and signed, was at the date hereof by (1)_____ signed as and declared to be his/her Will, in the presence of us who, at his/her request and in his/her presence, and in the presence of each other, have subscribed our names as witnesses thereto. Each of us observed the signing of this Will by (1)_____ and by each other subscribing witness and knows that each signature is the true signature of the person whose name was signed.

Each of us is now an adult and a competent witness and resides at the address set forth after his or her name.

We are acquainted with (1)_____. At this time, he/she is over the age of eighteen years, and to the best of our knowledge, he/she is of sound mind and is not acting under duress, menace, fraud, misrepresentation, or undue influence.

We declare under penalty of perjury that the foregoing is true and correct.

Executed on (38) _____at (39)_____, CA.

(41)_____Residing at (42)_____

_____

(43)_____ Residing at (44)_____

_____

Last Will and Testament

I, (1)_____, a resident of (2)_____ County, California, being of sound and disposing mind and memory and not acting under duress, menace, fraud or undue influence of any person whomsoever, do make, publish and declare this to be my Last Will and Testament, and I hereby expressly revoke all other wills, codicils, and testamentary writings heretofore made by me.

FIRST. I declare that I am married. My spouse's name is (4)_____. I have no children and no issue now living of a deceased child.

SECOND. I devise the following personal, tangible property to the follow persons:

(8)

I devise to (9)_____ all of my remaining personal effects, household furniture and furnishings, trailers, boats, pictures, works of art and art objects, collections, jewelry, silverware, wearing apparel, collections, sporting goods, and all other articles of household or personal use or ornament at whatsoever time acquired by me and wheresoever situated.

I devise to the following persons the cash amount listed after their respective names:

(10)

I devise to the following persons the real property described after their respective names. (12) Said real property is given free of all encumbrances or liens thereon.

(11)

I devise all of the rest, residue and remainder of my estate, real, personal and mixed, of whatsoever kind or character and wheresoever situated, of which I die possessed or to which I may in any manner be entitled, to (16) in the pro-portions listed after their names (17) in equal shares.

(18)

In the event any of the above named persons should predecease me or fail to survive me then his or her share shall lapse unless I have specifically named a person to take said bequest in the event of the first beneficiary's death.

Any beneficiary above who fails to survive me by thirty days shall be deemed to have predeceased me.

THIRD. I have intentionally and with full knowledge omitted to provide for my issue, ancestors, relatives and heirs living at the time of my demise, except for such provisions as are made specifically herein.

If any person who is or claims under or through a beneficiary of this Will, or if any person who would be entitled to share in my estate if I died intestate, should in any manner whatsoever, directly or indirectly, attack, contest or seek to impair or invalidate in court any provision of the following:

A. This Will or any Codicil to this Will;

B. Any revocable or irrevocable Trust established by me;

C. Any beneficiary designation executed by me with respect to any insurance policy, any "totten trust" account, any joint tenancy, any "transfer on death" account or any pension plan, or conspire or cooperate with anyone attempting to do any of the actions or things aforesaid, then I hereby specifically disinherit each such person and any devise, share or interest in my estate otherwise given to each such person under this Will or to which each such person might be entitled by law, is hereby revoked and shall pass and be distributed as though each such person had predeceased me leaving no issue or heirs whatsoever.

Any and every individual who asserts, or conspires or cooperates with any person who asserts, any claim against my Estate based on:

D. "Quantum meruit" theory;

E. Common law marriage, Marvin v. Marvin, 18 Cal. 3d 660 (1976) type of agreement or similar theory;

F. Constructive trust theory; or,

G. Oral agreement or written agreement which is to be proved by parole evidence, claiming that I agreed to gift or devise anything to such person or to pay such person or another for services rendered, regardless of whether a court may find that such agreement existed, then I hereby specifically disinherit each such person and any devise, share or interest in my estate otherwise given to each such person under this Will or to which each such person might be entitled by law, is hereby revoked and shall pass and be distributed as though each such person had predeceased me leaving no issue or heirs whatsoever.

FOURTH: I nominate and appoint (34)_____ as (35)_____
Executor hereunder (36) without bond. In the event he/she or both of them should decline, become unable or, for any reason, cease to serve as Executor then I nominate and appoint (37) _____ as Executor hereunder (36) without bond.

I authorize my Executor to sell, at either public or private sale, encumber or lease any property belonging to my estate, either with or without public notice, subject to such confirmation as may be required by law, and to hold, manage and operate any such property.

FIFTH. All handwritten "fill-ins" where directed above were made before the execution of this Will and are not initialed by me. All inter-lineations were made before the execution of this Will and are initialed by me.

The masculine, feminine, and neuter gender and the singular or plural number, shall each be deemed to include the others whenever the context so indicates.

IN WITNESS WHEREOF, I have hereunto set my hand this (38)_____ at (39) _____, CA.

(40)_____

The foregoing instrument, consisting of three pages, including the page on which this attestation clause is completed and signed, was at the date hereof by (1)_____ signed as and declared to be his/her Will, in the presence of us who, at his/her request and in his/her presence, and in the presence of each other, have subscribed our names as witnesses thereto. Each of us observed the signing of this Will by (1)_____ and by each other subscribing witness and knows that each signature is the true signature of the person whose name was signed.

Each of us is now an adult and a competent witness and resides at the address set forth after his or her name.

We are acquainted with (1)_____. At this time, he/she is over the age of eighteen years, and to the best of our knowledge, he/she is of sound mind and is not acting under duress, menace, fraud, misrepresentation, or undue influence.

We declare under penalty of perjury that the foregoing is true and correct.

Executed on (38)_____ at (39)_____, CA.

(41)_____ Residing at (42) _____

_____

(43)_____ Residing at (44) _____

_____

This page intentionally left blank.

Last Will and Testament

I, (1)_____, a resident of (2)_____ County, California, being of sound and disposing mind and memory and not acting under duress, menace, fraud or undue influence of any person whomsoever, do make, publish and declare this to be my Last Will and Testament, and I hereby expressly revoke all other wills, codicils, and testamentary writings heretofore made by me.

FIRST. I declare that I am (3) _____. My spouse's name was (4)_____. I have the following children:

(5)

I have a deceased child who left the following issue now surviving:

(6)

I have no other children and (7)_____ deceased children who left issue now surviving.

SECOND. I devise the following personal, tangible property to the follow persons:

(8)

I devise to (9) _____ all of my remaining personal effects, household furniture and furnishings, trailers, boats, pictures, works of art and art objects, collections, jewelry, silverware, wearing apparel, collections, sporting goods, and all other articles of household or personal use or ornament at whatsoever time acquired by me and wheresoever situated.

I devise to the following persons the cash amount listed after their respective names:

(10)

I devise to the following persons the real property described after their respective names. (12) Said real property is given free of all encumbrances or liens thereon.

(11)

I devise all of the rest, residue and remainder of my estate, real, personal and mixed, of whatsoever kind or character and wheresoever situated, of which I die possessed or to which I may in any manner be entitled, to (16) in the pro-portions listed after their names (17) or in equal shares.

(18)

In the event any of the above named persons should predecease me or fail to survive me then his or her share shall lapse unless I have specifically named a person to take said bequest in the event of the first beneficiary's death.

Any beneficiary above who fails to survive me by thirty days shall be deemed to have predeceased me.

THIRD. I have intentionally and with full knowledge omitted to provide for my issue, ancestors, relatives and heirs living at the time of my demise, except for such provisions as are made specifically herein.

If any person who is or claims under or through a beneficiary of this Will, or if any person who would be entitled to share in my estate if I died intestate, should in any manner whatsoever, directly or indirectly, attack, contest or seek to impair or invalidate in court any provision of the following:

A. This Will or any Codicil to this Will;

B. Any revocable or irrevocable Trust established by me;

C. Any beneficiary designation executed by me with respect to any insurance policy, any "totten trust" account, any joint tenancy, any "transfer on death" account or any pension plan, or conspire or cooperate with anyone attempting to do any of the actions or things aforesaid, then I hereby specifically disinherit each such person and any devise, share or interest in my estate otherwise given to each such person under this Will or to which each such person might be entitled by law, is hereby revoked and shall pass and be distributed as though each such person had predeceased me leaving no issue or heirs whatsoever.

Any and every individual who asserts, or conspires or cooperates with any person who asserts, any claim against my Estate based on:

D. "Quantum meruit" theory;

E. Common law marriage, Marvin v. Marvin, 18 Cal. 3d 660 (1976) type of agreement or similar theory;

F. Constructive trust theory; or,

G. Oral agreement or written agreement which is to be proved by parole evidence, claiming that I agreed to gift or devise anything to such person or to pay such person or another for services rendered, regardless of whether a court may find that such agreement existed, then I hereby specifically disinherit each such person and any devise, share or interest in my estate otherwise given to each such person under this Will or to which each such person might be entitled by law, is hereby revoked and shall pass and be distributed as though each such person had predeceased me leaving no issue or heirs whatsoever.

FOURTH: I nominate and appoint (34) _____ as (35)_____ Executor hereunder (36) without bond. In the event he/she/they should decline, become unable or, for any reason, cease to serve as Executor then I nominate and appoint (37) _____ as Executor hereunder (36) without bond.

I authorize my Executor to sell, at either public or private sale, encumber or lease any property belonging to my estate, either with or without public notice, subject to such confirmation as may be required by law, and to hold, manage and operate any such property.

FIFTH. All handwritten "fill-ins" where directed above were made before the execution of this Will and are not initialed by me. All inter-lineations were made before the execution of this Will and are initialed by me.

The masculine, feminine, and neuter gender and the singular or plural number, shall each be deemed to include the others whenever the context so indicates.

IN WITNESS WHEREOF, I have hereunto set my hand this (38)_____ at (39) _____, CA.

(40)_____

The foregoing instrument, consisting of four pages, including the page on which this attestation clause is completed and signed, was at the date hereof by (1)_____ signed as and declared to be his/her Will, in the presence of us who, at his/her request and in his/her presence, and in the presence of each other, have subscribed our names as witnesses thereto. Each of us observed the signing of this Will by (1)_____ and by each other subscribing witness and knows that each signature is the true signature of the person whose name was signed.

Each of us is now an adult and a competent witness and resides at the address set forth after his or her name.

We are acquainted with (1)_____. At this time, he/she is over the age of eighteen years, and to the best of our knowledge, he/she is of sound mind and is not acting under duress, menace, fraud, misrepresentation, or undue influence.

We declare under penalty of perjury that the foregoing is true and correct.

Executed on (38)_____ at (39)_____, CA.

(41)_____ Residing at (42) _____

_____

(43)_____ Residing at (44) _____

_____

Last Will and Testament

I, (1)_____, a resident of (2)_____ County, California, being of sound and disposing mind and memory and not acting under duress, menace, fraud or undue influence of any person whomsoever, do make, publish and declare this to be my Last Will and Testament, and I hereby expressly revoke all other wills, codicils, and testamentary writings heretofore made by me.

FIRST. I declare that I am (3)_____. My spouse's name was (4)_____. I have the following children:

(5)

I have a deceased child who left the following issue now surviving:

(6)

I have no other children and (7)_____ deceased children who left issue now surviving.

SECOND. I devise all of estate to the Custodian under the Uniform Gift to Minors Act hereinafter named, to have and to hold upon the purposes and conditions of said act. I am secure in the knowledge that said Custodian will retain those items of personal use or sentimental value for my child or children in a manner I have made known or will make known to said Custodian.

My Executor, in making distribution to the Custodian, shall allocate the estate properties into as many shares as I have children then living and children then deceased who left issue then living. One such equal share shall be set aside for each of my children then living and one such equal share shall be set aside for the issue then living, by right of representation, of each of my children who are then deceased but left issue then living.

The Custodian may deposit any portion of a child's share in an IRC 529 college savings plan for the benefit of said child.

Upon each child attaining the age of (29) _____ years, the Custodian shall deliver to said minor all of the remainder of his or her share.

In the event a child should die before distribution to him or her of his or her share, his or her share on hand at the time of his death shall thereupon be apportioned and distributed to his or her surviving issue, by right of representation. If such child should die before complete distribution to him or her of his or her share and leave no surviving issue, then the balance of the share then on hand shall go and be distributed to my heirs to be determined according to the laws of the State of California then in effect relating to the intestate succession of separate property not acquired from a predeceased spouse.

Each beneficiary hereunder is hereby prohibited from anticipating, encumbering, assigning, or in any other manner alienating his or her interest in either income or principal, and is without power so to do, nor shall such interest be subject to his or her liabilities or obligations, nor to attachment, execution, or other legal processes, bankruptcy proceedings or claims of creditors or others. The Trustee may, however, deposit in any bank designated in writing by a beneficiary, to his or her credit, income or principal payable to such beneficiary.

I nominate and appoint (30)_____ as Custodian hereunder (32) without bond. In the event he/she/they should decline to act, or for any other reason, is unable to act as Custodian then I appoint (33) _____ as Custodian hereunder without bond.

THIRD: I have intentionally and with full knowledge omitted to provide for my issue, ancestors, relatives and heirs living at the time of my demise, except for such provisions as are made specifically herein.

If any person who is or claims under or through a beneficiary of this Will, or if any person who would be entitled to share in my estate if I died intestate, should in any manner whatsoever, directly or indirectly, attack, contest or seek to impair or invalidate in court any provision of the following:

A. This Will or any Codicil to this Will;

B. Any revocable or irrevocable Trust established by me;

C. Any beneficiary designation executed by me with respect to any insurance policy, any "totten trust" account, any joint tenancy, any "transfer on death" account or any pension plan, or conspire or cooperate with anyone attempting to do any of the actions or things aforesaid, then I hereby specifically disinherit each such person and any devise, share or interest in my estate otherwise given to each such person under this Will or to which each such person might be entitled by law, is hereby revoked and shall pass and be distributed as though each such person had predeceased me leaving no issue or heirs whatsoever.

Any and every individual who asserts, or conspires or cooperates with any person who asserts, any claim against my Estate based on:

D. "Quantum meruit" theory;

E. Common law marriage, Marvin v. Marvin, 18 Cal. 3d 660 (1976) type of agreement or similar theory;

F. Constructive trust theory; or,

G. Oral agreement or written agreement which is to be proved by parole evidence, claiming that I agreed to gift or devise anything to such person or to pay such person or another for services rendered, regardless of whether a court may find that such agreement existed, then I hereby specifically disinherit each such person and any devise, share or interest in my estate otherwise given to each such person under this Will or to which each such person might be entitled by law, is hereby revoked and shall pass and be distributed as though each such person had predeceased me leaving no issue or heirs whatsoever.

FOURTH: I nominate and appoint (34) _____ as (35)_____ Executor hereunder (36) without bond. In the event he/she/they should decline, become unable or, for any reason, cease to serve as Executor then I nominate and appoint (37) _____ as Executor hereunder (36) without bond.

I authorize my Executor to sell, at either public or private sale, encumber or lease any property belonging to my estate, either with or without public notice, subject to such confirmation as may be required by law, and to hold, manage and operate any such property.

FIFTH. All typed and handwritten "fill-ins" where directed above were made before the execution of this Will and are not initialed by me. All crossed through words and inter-lineations were made before the execution of this Will and are initialed by me.

The masculine, feminine, and neuter gender and the singular or plural number, shall each be deemed to include the others whenever the context so indicates.

IN WITNESS WHEREOF, I have hereunto set my hand this (38)_____ at (39) _____, CA.

(40)_____

The foregoing instrument, consisting of four pages, including the page on which this attestation clause is completed and signed, was at the date hereof by (1)_____ signed as and declared to be his/her Will, in the presence of us who, at his/her request and in his/her presence, and in the presence of each other, have subscribed our names as witnesses thereto. Each of us observed the signing of this Will by (1)_____ and by each other subscribing witness and knows that each signature is the true signature of the person whose name was signed.

Each of us is now an adult and a competent witness and resides at the address set forth after his or her name.

We are acquainted with (1)_____. At this time, he/she is over the age of eighteen years, and to the best of our knowledge, he/she is of sound mind and is not acting under duress, menace, fraud, misrepresentation, or undue influence.

We declare under penalty of perjury that the foregoing is true and correct.

Executed on (38)_____ at (39)_____, CA.

(41)_____ Residing at (42) _____

_____

(43)_____ Residing at (44) _____

_____

Last Will and Testament

I, (1)_____, a resident of (2)_____ County, California, being of sound and disposing mind and memory and not acting under duress, menace, fraud or undue influence of any person whomsoever, do make, publish and declare this to be my Last Will and Testament, and I hereby expressly revoke all other wills, codicils, and testamentary writings heretofore made by me.

FIRST. I declare that I am (3) _____. My spouse's name was (4)_____. I have the following children:

(5)

I have a deceased child who left the following issue now surviving:

(6)

I have no other children and (7)_____ deceased children who left issue now surviving.

SECOND. I devise the following personal, tangible property to the follow persons:

(8)

I devise to (9) _____ all of my remaining personal effects, household furniture and furnishings, trailers, boats, pictures, works of art and art objects, collections, jewelry, silverware, wearing apparel, collections, sporting goods, and all other articles of household or personal use or ornament at whatsoever time acquired by me and wheresoever situated.

I devise to the following persons the cash amount listed after their respective names:

(10)

I devise to the following persons the real property described after their respective names. (12) Said real property is given free of all encumbrances or liens thereon.

(11)

I devise to (13)_____ a life estate in the following property located at: (14)_____. After the death of (13)_____ said property shall go, outright, to (15) _____ as the remainder person(s).

I devise all of the rest, residue and remainder of my estate, real, personal and mixed, of whatsoever kind or character and wheresoever situated, of which I die possessed or to which I may in any manner be entitled, to the following persons or entities (16) in the proportions listed after their names (17) in equal shares.

(18)

In the event any of the above named persons should predecease me or fail to survive me then his or her share shall lapse unless I have specifically named a person to take said bequest in the event of the first beneficiary's death.

Any beneficiary above who fails to survive me by thirty days shall be deemed to have predeceased me.

THIRD. I have intentionally and with full knowledge omitted to provide for my issue, ancestors, relatives and heirs living at the time of my demise, except for such provisions as are made specifically herein.

If any person who is or claims under or through a beneficiary of this Will, or if any person who would be entitled to share in my estate if I died intestate, should in any manner whatsoever, directly or indirectly, attack, contest or seek to impair or invalidate in court any provision of the following:

A. This Will or any Codicil to this Will;

B. Any revocable or irrevocable Trust established by me;

C. Any beneficiary designation executed by me with respect to any insurance policy, any "totten trust" account, any joint tenancy, any "transfer on death" account or any pension plan, or conspire or cooperate with anyone attempting to do any of the actions or things aforesaid, then I hereby specifically disinherit each such person and any devise, share or interest in my estate otherwise given to each such person under this Will or to which each such person might be entitled by law, is hereby revoked and shall pass and be distributed as though each such person had predeceased me leaving no issue or heirs whatsoever.

Any and every individual who asserts, or conspires or cooperates with any person who asserts, any claim against my Estate based on:

D. "Quantum meruit" theory;

E. Common law marriage, Marvin v. Marvin, 18 Cal. 3d 660 (1976) type of agreement or similar theory;

F. Constructive trust theory; or,

G. Oral agreement or written agreement which is to be proved by parole evidence, claiming that I agreed to gift or devise anything to such person or to pay such person or another for services rendered, regardless of whether a court may find that such agreement existed, then I hereby specifically disinherit each such person and any devise, share or interest in my estate otherwise given to each such person under this Will or to which each such person might be entitled by law, is hereby revoked and shall pass and be distributed as though each such person had predeceased me leaving no issue or heirs whatsoever.

FOURTH: I nominate and appoint (34) _____ as (35) _____ Executor hereunder (36) without bond. In the event he/she/they should decline, become unable or, for any reason, cease to serve as Executor then I nominate and appoint (37) _____ as Executor hereunder (36) without bond.

I authorize my Executor to sell, at either public or private sale, encumber or lease any property belonging to my estate, either with or without public notice, subject to such confirmation as may be required by law, and to hold, manage and operate any such property.

FIFTH. All type and handwritten "fill-ins" where directed above were made before the execution of this Will and are not initialed by me. All crossed through words and inter-lineations were made before the execution of this Will and are initialed by me.

Except as provided otherwise herein, the masculine, feminine, and neuter gender and the singular or plural number, shall each be deemed to include the others whenever the context so indicates.

IN WITNESS WHEREOF, I have hereunto set my hand this (38)_____ at (39) _____, CA.

(40)_____

The foregoing instrument, consisting of four pages, including the page on which this attestation clause is completed and signed, was at the date hereof by (1)_____ signed as and declared to be his/her Will, in the presence of us who, at his/her request and in his/her presence, and in the presence of each other, have subscribed our names as witnesses thereto. Each of us observed the signing of this Will by (1)_____ and by each other subscribing witness and knows that each signature is the true signature of the person whose name was signed.

Each of us is now an adult and a competent witness and resides at the address set forth after his or her name.

We are acquainted with (1)_____. At this time, he/she is over the age of eighteen years, and to the best of our knowledge, he/she is of sound mind and is not acting under duress, menace, fraud, misrepresentation, or undue influence.

We declare under penalty of perjury that the foregoing is true and correct.

Executed on (38)_____ at (39)_____, CA.

(41)_____Residing at (42)_____

_____

(43)_____ Residing at (44)_____

_____

Last Will and Testament

I, (1)_____, a resident of (2)_____ County, California, being of sound and disposing mind and memory and not acting under duress, menace, fraud or undue influence of any person whomsoever, do make, publish and declare this to be my Last Will and Testament, and I hereby expressly revoke all other wills, codicils, and testamentary writings heretofore made by me.

FIRST. I declare that I am (3) _____. My spouse's name was (4)_____. I have the following children:

(5)

I have a deceased child who left the following issue now surviving:

(6)

I have no other children and (7)_____ deceased children who left issue now surviving.

SECOND. I devise all of estate to the Trustee hereinafter named, to have and to hold upon the uses, trusts, purposes and conditions hereinafter provided. I am secure in the knowledge that my Trustee will retain those items of personal use or sentimental value for my child or children in a manner I have made known or will make known to my Trustee.

My Executor, in making distribution to the Trustee, shall allocate the trust properties into as many shares as I have children then living and children then deceased who left issue then living. One such equal share shall be set aside for each of my children then living and one such equal share shall be set aside for the issue then living, by right of representation, of each of my children who are then deceased but left issue then living. Said shares shall be held, administered, and distributed as provided in the following sections:

Each share set aside for a child of mine shall be held, administered and delivered for and to such beneficiary as follows:

1. The net income from the trust while said beneficiary is under 19 years of age and not a high school graduate shall be added to principal, from which the Trustee shall pay to or for the benefit of such beneficiary such sums as in the Trustee's discretion the Trustee shall deem necessary for such beneficiary's proper care, comfort, maintenance, support or education.

In making payments for the benefit of any beneficiary pursuant to this section 1, the Trustee shall construe his authority liberally to permit payments reasonably necessary to ease the financial burden on the guardian of the person of such beneficiary or other suitable individual with whom they reside, and on his family, resulting from such beneficiary's presence in his household.

2. Upon the beneficiary reaching 19 years of age or finishing high school(whichever occurs first), the Trustee shall pay to or apply for his or her benefit, from his or her trust, as much of the trust principal as the Trustee, in the Trustee's discretion, considers appropriate pursuant to sections 3 and 4 following.

3. After the beneficiary attains 19 years of age or finishes high school (whichever occurs first), the Trustee may, in the Trustee's discretion, pay to or apply from her trust, such amounts necessary for her education. For purposes hereof, education shall mean enrollment, attendance, and satisfactory progression towards a degree as a student at a recognized and accredited college, university, or similar institution of higher learning, including any graduate, professional school or college or trade school. Such educational payments and benefits shall include tuition, books, all direct educational costs and fees, and all reasonable living and transportation expenses. Payments hereunder shall be made during vacation periods within the regular school term under which the beneficiary is attending school and during "summer vacation" or similar vacation period between the regular school terms.

The Trustee may invest any portion of a beneficiary's trust share in an IRC 529 college savings plan for the benefit of said beneficiary.

4. If the beneficiary, his or her spouse, or any of his children should at any time or from time to time be in need, in the discretion of the Trustee, of funds due to illness, infirmity or other physical or mental disability or any emergency, the Trustee may relieve or contribute toward the relief of any such need or needs of the beneficiary by paying to him or her or using and applying for his or her benefit, such sum or sums out of the income and/or principal of his or her trust as the Trustee, in the Trustee's discretion, may deem necessary or advisable.

5. Upon the beneficiary attaining the age of 21 years, the Trustee shall begin to pay the beneficiary all of the net income, in monthly or other convenient installments, from the trust.

6. Upon the beneficiary attaining the age of (21)_____ years, the Trustee shall distribute and deliver to such beneficiary one-half of his trust estate. Upon each beneficiary attaining the age of (22)_____ years, the Trustee shall distribute and deliver to such beneficiary all of the remainder of his or her trust estate.

7. If, upon the attaining of the above ages, the Trustee suspects that said beneficiary may be abusing drugs and/or alcohol, the Trustee may require the beneficiary to take a reasonable drug and/or alcohol test. If the beneficiary fails said test, the trustee shall defer said principal payment to the beneficiary until the beneficiary passes said test. After a failed test, subsequent drug tests shall be administered at the request of the beneficiary but not less than six months after a prior test. In the event a beneficiary fails a drug and/or alcohol test, the

Trustee may use said beneficiary's trust estate to pay for a drug and/or alcohol abuse rehabilitation program and may require the beneficiary to enroll and to complete said program as a condition precedent to the taking of a subsequent drug and/or alcohol test.

8. In the event the beneficiary should die before complete distribution to him or her of his or her trust estate, his or her entire trust estate on hand at the time of his death shall thereupon be apportioned and distributed to his or her surviving issue, by right of representation. If such beneficiary should die before complete distribution to him or her of his or her trust estate and leave no surviving issue, then the balance of the trust estate then on hand shall go and be distributed to my heirs to be determined according to the laws of the State of California then in effect relating to the intestate succession of separate property not acquired from a predeceased spouse.

9. Each beneficiary hereunder is hereby prohibited from anticipating, encumbering, assigning, or in any other manner alienating his or her interest in either income or principal, and is without power so to do, nor shall such interest be subject to his or her liabilities or obligations, nor to attachment, execution, or other legal processes, bankruptcy proceedings or claims of creditors or others. The Trustee may, however, deposit in any bank designated in writing by a beneficiary, to his or her credit, income or principal payable to such beneficiary.

10. If, at any time, a trust created hereunder shall, in the sole judgment of the Trustee, be of the aggregate principal value of Fifty Thousand Dollars ($50,000.00) or less, the Trustee may, but need not, terminate such trust and distribute the assets thereof in the Trustee's possession to the beneficiary or beneficiaries, at the time of the current income thereof, and if there is more than one beneficiary, in the proportion in which they are beneficiaries.

11. I nominate and appoint (25)_____ as (26)_____ Trustee hereunder (27) without bond. In the event he/she or both of them should die, decline to act, or for any other reason, be unable to act as Trustee then I appoint (28)_____ as Trustee hereunder (27) without bond.

THIRD: I have intentionally and with full knowledge omitted to provide for my issue, ancestors, relatives and heirs living at the time of my demise, except for such provisions as are made specifically herein.

If any person who is or claims under or through a beneficiary of this Will, or if any person who would be entitled to share in my estate if I died intestate, should in any manner whatsoever, directly or indirectly, attack, contest or seek to impair or invalidate in court any provision of the following:

A. This Will or any Codicil to this Will;

B. Any revocable or irrevocable Trust established by me;

C. Any beneficiary designation executed by me with respect to any insurance policy, any "totten trust" account, any joint tenancy, any "transfer on death" account or any pension plan, or conspire or cooperate with anyone attempting to do any of the actions or things aforesaid, then I hereby specifically disinherit each such person and any devise, share or interest in my estate otherwise given to each such person under this Will or to which each such person might be entitled by law, is hereby revoked and shall pass and be distributed as though each such person had predeceased me leaving no issue or heirs whatsoever.

Any and every individual who asserts, or conspires or cooperates with any person who asserts, any claim against my Estate based on:

D. "Quantum meruit" theory;

E. Common law marriage, Marvin v. Marvin, 18 Cal. 3d 660 (1976) type of agreement or similar theory;

F. Constructive trust theory; or,

G. Oral agreement or written agreement which is to be proved by parole evidence, claiming that I agreed to gift or devise anything to such person or to pay such person or another for services rendered, regardless of whether a court may find that such agreement existed, then I hereby specifically disinherit each such person and any devise, share or interest in my estate otherwise given to each such person under this Will or to which each such person might be entitled by law, is hereby revoked and shall pass and be distributed as though each such person had predeceased me leaving no issue or heirs whatsoever.

FOURTH: I nominate and appoint (34) _____ as (35)_____ Executor hereunder (36) without bond. In the event he/she or both of them should decline, become unable or, for any reason, cease to serve as Executor then I nominate and appoint (37)_____ as Executor hereunder (36) without bond.

I authorize my Executor to sell, at either public or private sale, encumber or lease any property belonging to my estate, either with or without public notice, subject to such confirmation as may be required by law, and to hold, manage and operate any such property.

FIFTH. All typed and handwritten "fill-ins" where directed above were made before the execution of this Will and are not initialed by me. All crossed through words and inter-lineations were made before the execution of this Will and are initialed by me.

The masculine, feminine, and neuter gender and the singular or plural number, shall each be deemed to include the others whenever the context so indicates.

IN WITNESS WHEREOF, I have hereunto set my hand this (38)_____ at (39) _____, CA.

OR

3.a. (47 - Option 2 Start) In addition to any other payments to the beneficiary hereunder, the Trustee shall, upon the written request of the beneficiary in December of each calendar year, pay to the beneficiary amounts from principal that the beneficiary requests, not exceeding in any single calendar year the greater of the following amounts: $5,000.00 or 5 percent of the value of the principal of the beneficiary's trust estate; determined as of the end of the calendar year. This right of withdrawal is noncumulative, so that if the beneficiary does not withdraw the full amount permitted to be withdrawn during any calendar year, the right to withdraw the remaining amount will lapse at the end of the calendar year.

b. On the death of the beneficiary his or her entire trust estate on hand at the time of his death shall thereupon be apportioned and distributed to:

(23)_____ if (23)_____is then deceased then the trust estate then on hand shall go to (24)_____. (47 - Option 2A End)

OR:

the beneficiary's surviving issue, by right of representation. If such beneficiary should die before complete distribution to him or her of his or her trust estate and leave no surviving issue, then the balance of the trust estate then on hand shall go and be distributed to my heirs to be determined according to the laws of the State of California then in effect relating to the intestate succession of separate property not acquired from a predeceased spouse. (47 - Option 2B End)

4. Each beneficiary hereunder is hereby prohibited from anticipating, encumbering, assigning, or in any other manner alienating his or her interest in either income or principal, and is without power so to do, nor shall such interest be subject to his or her liabilities or obligations, nor to attachment, execution, or other legal processes, bankruptcy proceedings or claims of creditors or others. The Trustee may, however, deposit in any bank designated in writing by a beneficiary, to his or her credit, income or principal payable to such beneficiary.

5. If, at any time, a trust created hereunder shall, in the sole judgment of the Trustee, be of the aggregate principal value of Fifty Thousand Dollars ($50,000.00) or less, the Trustee may, but need not, terminate such trust and distribute the assets thereof in the Trustee's possession to the beneficiary or beneficiaries, at the time of the current income thereof, and if there is more than one beneficiary, in the proportion in which they are beneficiaries.

6. I nominate and appoint (25)_____ as (26) _____ Trustee hereunder (27) without bond. In the event he/she/or bot of them should die, decline to act, or for any other reason, be unable to act as Trustee then I appoint (28) _____ as Trustee hereunder (27) without bond.

THIRD: I have intentionally and with full knowledge omitted to provide for my issue, ancestors, relatives and heirs living at the time of my demise, except for such provisions as are made specifically herein.

If any person who is or claims under or through a beneficiary of this Will, or if any person who would be entitled to share in my estate if I died intestate, should in any manner whatsoever, directly or indirectly, attack, contest or seek to impair or invalidate in court any provision of the following:

A. This Will or any Codicil to this Will;

B. Any revocable or irrevocable Trust established by me;

C. Any beneficiary designation executed by me with respect to any insurance policy, any "totten trust" account, any joint tenancy, any "transfer on death" account or any pension plan, or conspire or cooperate with anyone attempting to do any of the actions or things aforesaid, then I hereby specifically disinherit each such person and any devise, share or interest in my estate otherwise given to each such person under this Will or to which each such person might be entitled by law, is hereby revoked and shall pass and be distributed as though each such person had predeceased me leaving no issue or heirs whatsoever.

Any and every individual who asserts, or conspires or cooperates with any person who asserts, any claim against my Estate based on:

D. "Quantum meruit" theory;

E. Common law marriage, Marvin v. Marvin, 18 Cal. 3d 660 (1976) type of agreement or similar theory;

F. Constructive trust theory; or,

G. Oral agreement or written agreement which is to be proved by parole evidence, claiming that I agreed to gift or devise anything to such person or to pay such person or another for services rendered, regardless of whether a court may find that such agreement existed, then I hereby specifically disinherit each such person and any devise, share or interest in my estate otherwise given to each such person under this Will or to which each such person might be entitled by law, is hereby revoked and shall pass and be distributed as though each such person had predeceased me leaving no issue or heirs whatsoever.

FOURTH: I nominate and appoint (34) _____ as (35) _____ Executor hereunder (36) without bond. In the event he/she/or both of them should decline, become unable or, for any reason, cease to serve as Executor then I nominate and appoint (37) _____ as Executor hereunder (36) without bond.

I authorize my Executor to sell, at either public or private sale, encumber or lease any property belonging to my estate, either with or without public notice, subject to such confirmation as may be required by law, and to hold, manage and operate any such property.

FIFTH. All typed and handwritten "fill-ins" where directed above were made before the execution of this Will and are not initialed by me. All crossed through words and inter-lineations were made before the execution of this Will and are initialed by me.

Except as provided otherwise herein, the masculine, feminine, and neuter gender and the singular or plural number, shall each be deemed to include the others whenever the context so indicates.

IN WITNESS WHEREOF, I have hereunto set my hand this (38)_____
at (39) _____, CA.

(40)_____

The foregoing instrument, consisting of five pages, including the page on which this attestation clause is completed and signed, was at the date hereof by (40)_____ signed as and declared to be his/her Will, in the presence of us who, at his/her request and in his/her presence, and in the presence of each other, have subscribed our names as witnesses thereto. Each of us observed the signing of this Will by (40)_____ and by each other subscribing witness and knows that each signature is the true signature of the person whose name was signed.

Each of us is now an adult and a competent witness and resides at the address set forth after his or her name.

We are acquainted with (40)_____. At this time, he/she is over the age of eighteen years, and to the best of our knowledge, he/she is of sound mind and is not acting under duress, menace, fraud, misrepresentation, or undue influence.

We declare under penalty of perjury that the foregoing is true and correct.

Executed on (38) _____ at (39)_____, CA.

(41)_____Residing at (42)_____

_____

(43)_____ Residing at (44)_____

_____

This page intentionally left blank.

Last Will and Testament

I, (1)_____, a resident of (2)_____ County, California, being of sound and disposing mind and memory and not acting under duress, menace, fraud or undue influence of any person whomsoever, do make, publish and declare this to be my Last Will and Testament, and I hereby expressly revoke all other wills, codicils, and testamentary writings heretofore made by me.

FIRST. I declare that I am (3)_____. My spouse's name was (4)_____. I have no children, living and no deceased children who left issue now living.

SECOND. I devise the following personal, tangible property:

(8)

I devise to (9)_____ all of my remaining personal effects, household furniture and furnishings, trailers, boats, pictures, works of art and art objects, collections, jewelry, silverware, wearing apparel, collections, sporting goods, and all other articles of household or personal use or ornament at whatsoever time acquired by me and wheresoever situated.

I devise to the following persons the cash amount listed after their respective names:

(10)

I devise to the following persons the real property described after their respective names. (12) Said real property is given free of all encumbrances or liens thereon.

(11)

I devise to (13)_____ a life estate in the following property located at: (14)_____. After the death of (13)_____ said property shall go, outright, to (15) _____ as the remainder person(s).

I devise all of the rest, residue and remainder of my estate, real, personal and mixed, of whatsoever kind or character and wheresoever situated, of which I die possessed or to which I may in any manner be entitled, to the following persons or entities (16) in the proportions listed after their names (17) in equal shares.

(18)

In the event any of the above named persons should predecease me or fail to survive me then his or her share shall lapse unless I have specifically named a person to take said bequest in the event of the first beneficiary's death.

Any beneficiary above who fails to survive me by thirty days shall be deemed to have predeceased me.

THIRD: I have intentionally and with full knowledge omitted to provide for my issue, ancestors, relatives and heirs living at the time of my demise, except for such provisions as are made specifically herein.

If any person who is or claims under or through a beneficiary of this Will, or if any person who would be entitled to share in my estate if I died intestate, should in any manner whatsoever, directly or indirectly, attack, contest or seek to impair or invalidate in court any provision of the following:

A. This Will or any Codicil to this Will;

B. Any revocable or irrevocable Trust established by me;

C. Any beneficiary designation executed by me with respect to any insurance policy, any "totten trust" account, any joint tenancy, any "transfer on death" account or any pension plan, or conspire or cooperate with anyone attempting to do any of the actions or things aforesaid, then I hereby specifically disinherit each such person and any devise, share or interest in my estate otherwise given to each such person under this Will or to which each such person might be entitled by law, is hereby revoked and shall pass and be distributed as though each such person had predeceased me leaving no issue or heirs whatsoever.

Any and every individual who asserts, or conspires or cooperates with any person who asserts, any claim against my Estate based on:

D. "Quantum meruit" theory;

E. Common law marriage, Marvin v. Marvin, 18 Cal. 3d 660 (1976) type of agreement or similar theory;

F. Constructive trust theory; or,

G. Oral agreement or written agreement which is to be proved by parole evidence, claiming that I agreed to gift or devise anything to such person or to pay such person or another for services rendered, regardless of whether a court may find that such agreement existed, then I hereby specifically disinherit each such person and any devise, share or interest in my estate otherwise given to each such person under this Will or to which each such person might be entitled by law, is hereby revoked and shall pass and be distributed as though each such person had predeceased me leaving no issue or heirs whatsoever.

FOURTH: I nominate and appoint (34) _____ as (35)_____ Executor hereunder (36) without bond. In the event he/she/they should decline, become unable or, for any reason, cease to serve as Executor then I nominate and appoint (37) _____ as Executor hereunder (36) without bond.

I authorize my Executor to sell, at either public or private sale, encumber or lease any property belonging to my estate, either with or without public notice, subject to such confirmation as may be required by law, and to hold, manage and operate any such property.

FIFTH. All typed and handwritten "fill-ins" where directed above were made before the execution of this Will and are not initialed by me. All crossed through words inter-lineations were made before the execution of this Will and are initialed by me.

The masculine, feminine, and neuter gender and the singular or plural number, shall each be deemed to include the others whenever the context so indicates.

IN WITNESS WHEREOF, I have hereunto set my hand this (38)_____ at (39) _____, CA.

(40)_____

The foregoing instrument, consisting of four pages, including the page on which this attestation clause is completed and signed, was at the date hereof by (1)_____ signed as and declared to be his/her Will, in the presence of us who, at his/her request and in his/her presence, and in the presence of each other, have subscribed our names as witnesses thereto. Each of us observed the signing of this Will by (1)_____ and by each other subscribing witness and knows that each signature is the true signature of the person whose name was signed.

Each of us is now an adult and a competent witness and resides at the address set forth after his or her name.

We are acquainted with (1)_____. At this time, he/she is over the age of eighteen years, and to the best of our knowledge, he/she is of sound mind and is not acting under duress, menace, fraud, misrepresentation, or undue influence.

We declare under penalty of perjury that the foregoing is true and correct.

Executed on (38)_____ at (39)_____, CA.

(41)_____ Residing at (42)   _____

      _____

(43)_____ Residing at (44)   _____

      _____

Last Will and Testament

I, (1)_____, a resident of (2)_____ County, California, being of sound and disposing mind and memory and not acting under duress, menace, fraud or undue influence of any person whomsoever, do make, publish and declare this to be my Last Will and Testament, and I hereby expressly revoke all other wills, codicils, and testamentary writings heretofore made by me.

FIRST. I declare that I am (3)_____. My spouse's name was (4)_____. I have no children, living and no deceased children who left issue now living.

SECOND. I devise the following personal, tangible property to the follow persons:

(8)

I devise to (9)_____ all of my remaining personal effects, household furniture and furnishings, trailers, boats, pictures, works of art and art objects, collections, jewelry, silverware, wearing apparel, collections, sporting goods, and all other articles of household or personal use or ornament at whatsoever time acquired by me and wheresoever situated.

I devise to the following persons the cash amount listed after their respective names:

(10)

I devise to the following persons the real property described after their respective names. (12) Said real property is given free of all encumbrances or liens thereon.

(11)

I devise all of the rest, residue and remainder of my estate, real, personal and mixed, of whatsoever kind or character and wheresoever situated, of which I die possessed or to which I may in any manner be entitled, to (16) in the pro-portions listed after their names (17) in equal shares.

(18)

(19)_____ shares to the Trustee hereinafter named, to have and to hold for the benefit of (20)_____upon the uses, trusts, purposes and conditions hereinafter provided.

1. If the beneficiary, his or her spouse, or any of his children should at any time or from time to time be in need, in the discretion of the Trustee, of funds due to illness, infirmity or other physical or mental disability or any emergency, the Trustee may relieve or contribute toward the relief of any such need or needs of the beneficiary by paying to him or her or using and applying for his or her benefit, such sum or sums out of the income and/or principal of his or her trust as the Trustee, in the Trustee's discretion, may deem necessary or advisable.

2. The Trustee shall pay the beneficiary all of the net income, in monthly or other convenient installments, from the trust.

3.a. (47 - Option 1 Start) Upon the beneficiary attaining the age of (21)_____ years, the Trustee shall distribute and deliver to such beneficiary one-half of his trust estate. Upon the beneficiary attaining the age of (22)_____ years, the Trustee shall distribute and deliver to such beneficiary all of the remainder of his or her trust estate.

3.b. If, upon the attaining of the above ages, the Trustee suspects that said beneficiary may be abusing drugs and/or alcohol, the Trustee may require the beneficiary to take a reasonable drug and/or alcohol test. If the beneficiary fails said test, the trustee shall defer said principal payment to the beneficiary until the beneficiary passes said test. After a failed test, subsequent drug tests shall be administered at the request of the beneficiary but not less than six months after a prior test. In the event a beneficiary fails a drug and/or alcohol test, the Trustee may use said beneficiary's trust estate to pay for a drug and/or alcohol abuse rehabilitation program and may require the beneficiary to enroll and to complete said program as a condition precedent to the taking of a subsequent drug and/or alcohol test.

3.c. In the event the beneficiary should die before complete distribution to him or her of his or her trust estate, his or her entire trust estate on hand at the time of his death shall thereupon be apportioned and distributed to his or her surviving issue, by right of representation. If such beneficiary should die before complete distribution to him or her of his or her trust estate and leave no surviving issue, then the balance of the trust estate then on hand shall go and be distributed to my heirs to be determined according to the laws of the State of California then in effect relating to the intestate succession of separate property not acquired from a predeceased spouse. (47 - Option 1 End)

OR

3.a. (47 - Option 2 Start) In addition to any other payments to the beneficiary hereunder, the Trustee shall, upon the written request of the beneficiary in December of each calendar year, pay to the beneficiary amounts from principal that the beneficiary requests, not exceeding in any single calendar year the greater of the following amounts: $5,000.00 or 5 percent of the value of the principal of the beneficiary's trust estate; determined as of the end of the calendar year. This right of withdrawal is noncumulative, so that if the beneficiary does not withdraw the full amount permitted to be withdrawn during any calendar year, the right to withdraw the remaining amount will lapse at the end of the calendar year.

3.b.On the death of the beneficiary his or her entire trust estate on hand at the time of his death shall thereupon be apportioned and distributed to:

(23)_____ If (23)_____is then deceased then the trust estate then on hand shall go to (24)_____, if he is then living. (47 - Option 2A End)

OR:

the beneficiary's surviving issue, by right of representation. If such beneficiary should die before complete distribution to him or her of his or her trust estate and leave no surviving issue, then the balance of the trust estate then on hand shall go and be distributed to my heirs to be determined according to the laws of the State of California then in effect relating to the intestate succession of separate property not acquired from a predeceased spouse. (47 - Option 2B End)

4. Each beneficiary hereunder is hereby prohibited from anticipating, encumbering, assigning, or in any other manner alienating his or her interest in either income or principal, and is without power so to do, nor shall such interest be subject to his or her liabilities or obligations, nor to attachment, execution, or other legal processes, bankruptcy proceedings or claims of creditors or others. The Trustee may, however, deposit in any bank designated in writing by a beneficiary, to his or her credit, income or principal payable to such beneficiary.

5. If, at any time, a trust created hereunder shall, in the sole judgment of the Trustee, be of the aggregate principal value of Fifty Thousand Dollars ($50,000.00) or less, the Trustee may, but need not, terminate such trust and distribute the assets thereof in the Trustee's possession to the beneficiary or beneficiaries, at the time of the current income thereof, and if there is more than one beneficiary, in the proportion in which they are beneficiaries.

6. I nominate and appoint (25)_____ as (26)_____ Trustee hereunder (27) without bond. In the event he/she/they should die, decline to act, or for any other reason, be unable to act as Trustee then I appoint (28) _____ as Trustee hereunder (27) without bond.   7. In the event any of the above named persons should predecease me or fail to survive me then his or her share shall lapse unless I have specifically named a person to take said bequest in the event of the first beneficiary's death.

Any beneficiary above who fails to survive me by thirty days shall be deemed to have predeceased me.

THIRD: I have intentionally and with full knowledge omitted to provide for my issue, ancestors, relatives and heirs living at the time of my demise, except for such provisions as are made specifically herein.

If any person who is or claims under or through a beneficiary of this Will, or if any person who would be entitled to share in my estate if I died intestate, should in any manner whatsoever, directly or indirectly, attack, contest or seek to impair or invalidate in court any provision of the following:

A. This Will or any Codicil to this Will;

B. Any revocable or irrevocable Trust established by me;

C. Any beneficiary designation executed by me with respect to any insurance policy, any "totten trust" account, any joint tenancy, any "transfer on death" account or any pension plan, or conspire or cooperate with anyone attempting to do any of the actions or things aforesaid, then I hereby specifically disinherit each such person and any devise, share or interest in my estate otherwise given to each such person under this Will or to which each such person might be entitled by law, is hereby revoked and shall pass and be distributed as though each such person had predeceased me leaving no issue or heirs whatsoever.

Any and every individual who asserts, or conspires or cooperates with any person who asserts, any claim against my Estate based on:

D. "Quantum meruit" theory;

E. Common law marriage, Marvin v. Marvin, 18 Cal. 3d 660 (1976) type of agreement or similar theory;

F. Constructive trust theory; or,

G. Oral agreement or written agreement which is to be proved by parole evidence, claiming that I agreed to gift or devise anything to such person or to pay such person or another for services rendered, regardless of whether a court may find that such agreement existed, then I hereby specifically disinherit each such person and any devise, share or interest in my estate otherwise given to each such person under this Will or to which each such person might be entitled by law, is hereby revoked and shall pass and be distributed as though each such person had predeceased me leaving no issue or heirs whatsoever.

FOURTH: I nominate and appoint (34)_____ as (35)___Executor_ hereunder (36) without bond. In the event he/she/they should decline, become unable or, for any reason, cease to serve as Executor then I nominate and appoint (37) _____ as Executor hereunder (36) without bond.

I authorize my Executor to sell, at either public or private sale, encumber or lease any property belonging to my estate, either with or without public notice, subject to such confirmation as may be required by law, and to hold, manage and operate any such property.

FIFTH. All typed and handwritten "fill-ins" where directed above were made before the execution of this Will and are not initialed by me. All crossed through words and inter-lineations were made before the execution of this Will and are initialed by me.

The masculine, feminine, and neuter gender and the singular or plural number, shall each be deemed to include the others whenever the context so indicates.

IN WITNESS WHEREOF, I have hereunto set my hand this (38)_____ at (39) _____, CA.

(40)_____

The foregoing instrument, consisting of five pages, including the page on which this attestation clause is completed and signed, was at the date hereof by (1)_____ signed as and declared to be his/her Will, in the presence of us who, at his/her request and in his/her presence, and in the presence of each other, have subscribed our names as witnesses thereto. Each of us observed the signing of this Will by (1)_____ and by each other subscribing witness and knows that each signature is the true signature of the person whose name was signed.

Each of us is now an adult and a competent witness and resides at the address set forth after his or her name.

We are acquainted with (1)_____. At this time, he/she is over the age of eighteen years, and to the best of our knowledge, he/she is of sound mind and is not acting under duress, menace, fraud, misrepresentation, or undue influence.

We declare under penalty of perjury that the foregoing is true and correct.

Executed on (38)_____ at (39)_____, CA.

(41)_____ Residing at (42) _____

_____

(43)_____ Residing at (44) _____

_____

This page intentionally left blank.

Codicil to Last Will and Testament

I, (1)_____, a resident of (2)_____ County, California, being of sound and disposing mind and memory and not acting under duress, menace, fraud or undue influence of any person whomsoever, do make, publish and declare this to be the (31)_____ codicil to my Last Will and Testament dated (45)_____

1.   Paragraph _____ is amended as follows:

(46)

2. All typed and handwritten "fill-ins" where directed above were made before the execution of this Will and are not initialed by me. All crossed through words and inter-lineations were made before the execution of this Will and are initialed by me.

3. I hereby ratify, confirm and republish my said Last Will and Testament, as modified by this Codicil thereto.

IN WITNESS WHEREOF, I have hereunto set my hand this (38)_____ at (39) _____, CA.

(40)_____

The foregoing instrument, consisting of two pages, including the page on which this attestation clause is completed and signed, was at the date hereof by (1)_____ signed as and declared to be his/her Codicil, in the presence of us who, at his/her request and in his/her presence, and in the presence of each other, have subscribed our names as witnesses thereto. Each of us observed the signing of this Codicil by (1)_____ and by each other subscribing witness and knows that each signature is the true signature of the person whose name was signed.

Each of us is now an adult and a competent witness and resides at the address set forth after his or her name.

We are acquainted with (1)_____. At this time, he/she is over the age of eighteen years, and to the best of our knowledge, he/she is of sound mind and is not acting under duress, menace, fraud, misrepresentation, or undue influence.

We declare under penalty of perjury that the foregoing is true and correct.

Executed on (38)_____ at (39)_____, CA.

(41)_____Residing at (42)_____

_____

(43)_____ Residing at (44)_____

_____

INDEX

401(k), 4

A

animals, 18
annuity, 6, 13
appraisal, 28
Asset Roadmap, 15
assets, 1, 3–4, 5, 9–16, 33, 41
    not subject to disposition by will and passing
        without probate, 11–14
    subject to disposition by will, 9–10
    subject to disposition in a will but passing
        without probate , 11
attestation clause, 44, 45–46, 55

B

bank accounts, 4, 12
beneficiary, 1, 4, 13, 14, 15, 16, 20, 21, 22, 23, 29,
    30, 32, 33, 41
    disqualified, 21–22
bequest, 11, 27–34, 54
    conditions, 31–32
    definition of, 27
    residual, 27, 30
        shares, 30
    specific, 27, 28
brokerage accounts, 4

C

California Bar Association, 7
care custodian, 21, 22
caregiver, 6
certificate of independent review, 21, 22
charity, 18
codicil, 47, 48, 53
contest. *See will*
court, 1, 14, 18, 19, 20, 22, 28, 35, 36, 41, 46, 48,
    51, 53, 54
custodians, 19, 41. *See also trustee*
custodianship, 20

D

death certificate, 13
debts, 30, 54
dependent adult, 21, 22
devise. *See bequest*
disinheritance, 17, 23, 24
    clause, 23, 54
disqualified persons, 6, 17

E

estate, 11, 23, 29, 30, 33, 34, 38, 39, 41, 45
    plan, 15
executor, 28, 38–40, 41, 49, 53, 54
    court, 38
    definition of, 38
    statutory fee, 39
    trust company, 39

F

federal estate tax, 28, 33
federal gift tax, 12, 16
fiduciary, 35–42
    definition of, 35

G

guardian, 18–19, 35–38, 55
    court, 36, 37
    of the estate, 35
    of the person, 35

H

heirs. *See beneficiary*

SPHINX® PUBLISHING ORDER FORM

BILL TO:		SHIP TO:	
Phone #	Terms	F.O.B. Chicago, IL	Ship Date

Charge my: ☐ VISA   ☐ MasterCard   ☐ American Express

☐ **Money Order or Personal Check**

Credit Card Number ☐☐☐☐☐☐☐☐☐☐☐☐☐☐☐☐☐   Expiration Date

Qty	ISBN	Title	Retail	Ext.	Qty	ISBN	Title	Retail	Ext.
		SPHINX PUBLISHING NATIONAL TITLES				1-57248-186-2	Manual de Beneficios para el Seguro Social	$18.95	
	1-57248-148-X	Cómo Hacer su Propio Testamento	$16.95			1-57248-220-6	Mastering the MBE	$16.95	
	1-57248-226-5	Cómo Restablecer su propio Crédito y Renegociar sus Deudas	$21.95			1-57248-167-6	Most Valuable Bus. Legal Forms You'll Ever Need (3E)	$21.95	
	1-57248-147-1	Cómo Solicitar su Propio Divorcio	$24.95			1-57248-130-7	Most Valuable Personal Legal Forms You'll Ever Need	$24.95	
	1-57248-238-9	The 529 College Savings Plan	$16.95			1-57248-098-X	The Nanny and Domestic Help Legal Kit	$22.95	
	1-57248-166-8	The Complete Book of Corporate Forms	$24.95			1-57248-089-0	Neighbor v. Neighbor (2E)	$16.95	
	1-57248-229-X	The Complete Legal Guide to Senior Care	$21.95			1-57248-169-2	The Power of Attorney Handbook (4E)	$19.95	
	1-57248-201-X	The Complete Patent Book	$26.95			1-57248-149-8	Repair Your Own Credit and Deal with Debt	$18.95	
	1-57248-163-3	Crime Victim's Guide to Justice (2E)	$21.95			1-57248-217-6	Sexual Harassment: Your Guide to Legal Action	$18.95	
	1-57248-251-6	The Entrepreneur's Internet Handbook	$21.95			1-57248-219-2	The Small Business Owner's Guide to Bankruptcy	$21.95	
	1-57248-159-5	Essential Guide to Real Estate Contracts	$18.95			1-57248-168-4	The Social Security Benefits Handbook (3E)	$18.95	
	1-57248-160-9	Essential Guide to Real Estate Leases	$18.95			1-57248-216-8	Social Security Q&A	$12.95	
	1-57248-254-0	Family Limited Partnership	$26.95			1-57248-221-4	Teen Rights	$22.95	
	1-57248-139-0	Grandparents' Rights (3E)	$24.95			1-57248-236-2	Unmarried Parents' Rights (2E)	$19.95	
	1-57248-188-9	Guía de Inmigración a Estados Unidos (3E)	$24.95			1-57248-161-7	U.S.A. Immigration Guide (4E)	$24.95	
	1-57248-187-0	Guía de Justicia para Víctimas del Crimen	$21.95			1-57248-192-7	The Visitation Handbook	$18.95	
	1-57248-103-X	Help Your Lawyer Win Your Case (2E)	$14.95			1-57248-225-7	Win Your Unemployment Compensation Claim (2E)	$21.95	
	1-57248-164-1	How to Buy a Condominium or Townhome (2E)	$19.95			1-57248-138-2	Winning Your Personal Injury Claim (2E)	$24.95	
	1-57248-191-9	How to File Your Own Bankruptcy (5E)	$21.95			1-57248-162-5	Your Right to Child Custody, Visitation and Support (2E)	$24.95	
	1-57248-132-3	How to File Your Own Divorce (4E)	$24.95			1-57248-157-9	Your Rights When You Owe Too Much	$16.95	
	1-57248-083-1	How to Form a Limited Liability Company	$22.95				**CALIFORNIA TITLES**		
	1-57248-231-1	How to Form a Nonprofit Corporation (2E)	$24.95			1-57248-150-1	CA Power of Attorney Handbook (2E)	$18.95	
	1-57248-133-1	How to Form Your Own Corporation (3E)	$24.95			1-57248-151-X	How to File for Divorce in CA (3E)	$26.95	
	1-57248-224-9	How to Form Your Own Partnership (2E)	$24.95			1-57248-145-5	How to Probate and Settle an Estate in California	$26.95	
	1-57248-232-X	How to Make Your Own Simple Will (3E)	$18.95			1-57248-146-3	How to Start a Business in CA	$18.95	
	1-57248-200-1	How to Register Your Own Copyright (4E)	$24.95			1-57248-194-3	How to Win in Small Claims Court in CA (2E)	$18.95	
	1-57248-104-8	How to Register Your Own Trademark (3E)	$21.95			1-57248-246-X	Make Your Own CA Will	$18.95	
	1-57248-233-8	How to Write Your Own Living Will (3E)	$18.95			1-57248-196-X	The Landlord's Legal Guide in CA	$24.95	
	1-57248-156-0	How to Write Your Own Premarital Agreement (3E)	$24.95			1-57248-241-9	Tenants' Rights in CA	$21.95	
	1-57248-230-3	Incorporate in Delaware from Any State	$24.95				**FLORIDA TITLES**		
	1-57248-158-7	Incorporate in Nevada from Any State	$24.95			1-57071-363-4	Florida Power of Attorney Handbook (2E)	$16.95	
	1-57248-250-8	Inmigración a los EE.UU. Paso a Paso	$22.95			1-57248-176-5	How to File for Divorce in FL (7E)	$26.95	
	1-57071-333-2	Jurors' Rights (2E)	$12.95			1-57248-177-3	How to Form a Corporation in FL (5E)	$24.95	
	1-57248-223-0	Legal Research Made Easy (3E)	$21.95			1-57248-203-6	How to Form a Limited Liability Co. in FL (2E)	$24.95	
	1-57248-165-X	Living Trusts and Other Ways to Avoid Probate (3E)	$24.95			1-57071-401-0	How to Form a Partnership in FL	$22.95	

Form Continued on Following Page   **SUBTOTAL**

To order, call Sourcebooks at 1-800-432-7444 or FAX (630) 961-2168 (Bookstores, libraries, wholesalers—please call for discount)

Prices are subject to change without notice.

Find more legal information at: www.SphinxLegal.com

SPHINX® PUBLISHING ORDER FORM

Qty	ISBN	Title	Retail	Ext.
____	1-57248-113-7	How to Make a FL Will (6E)	$16.95	____
____	1-57248-088-2	How to Modify Your FL Divorce Judgment (4E)	$24.95	____
____	1-57248-144-7	How to Probate and Settle an Estate in FL (4E)	$26.95	____
____	1-57248-081-5	How to Start a Business in FL (5E)	$16.95	____
____	1-57248-204-4	How to Win in Small Claims Court in FL (7E)	$18.95	____
____	1-57248-202-8	Land Trusts in Florida (6E)	$29.95	____
____	1-57248-123-4	Landlords' Rights and Duties in FL (8E)	$21.95	____

GEORGIA TITLES

Qty	ISBN	Title	Retail	Ext.
____	1-57248-137-4	How to File for Divorce in GA (4E)	$21.95	____
____	1-57248-180-3	How to Make a GA Will (4E)	$21.95	____
____	1-57248-140-4	How to Start a Business in Georgia (2E)	$16.95	____

ILLINOIS TITLES

Qty	ISBN	Title	Retail	Ext.
____	1-57248-244-3	Child Custody, Visitation, and Support in IL	$24.95	____
____	1-57248-206-0	How to File for Divorce in IL (3E)	$24.95	____
____	1-57248-170-6	How to Make an IL Will (3E)	$16.95	____
____	1-57248-247-8	How to Start a Business in IL (3E)	$21.95	____
____	1-57248-252-4	The Landlord's Legal Guide in IL	$24.95	____

MASSACHUSETTS TITLES

Qty	ISBN	Title	Retail	Ext.
____	1-57248-128-5	How to File for Divorce in MA (3E)	$24.95	____
____	1-57248-115-3	How to Form a Corporation in MA	$24.95	____
____	1-57248-108-0	How to Make a MA Will (2E)	$16.95	____
____	1-57248-248-6	How to Start a Business in MA (3E)	$21.95	____
____	1-57248-209-5	The Landlord's Legal Guide in MA	$24.95	____

MICHIGAN TITLES

Qty	ISBN	Title	Retail	Ext.
____	1-57248-215-X	How to File for Divorce in MI (3E)	$24.95	____
____	1-57248-182-X	How to Make a MI Will (3E)	$16.95	____
____	1-57248-183-8	How to Start a Business in MI (3E)	$18.95	____

MINNESOTA TITLES

Qty	ISBN	Title	Retail	Ext.
____	1-57248-142-0	How to File for Divorce in MN	$21.95	____
____	1-57248-179-X	How to Form a Corporation in MN	$24.95	____
____	1-57248-178-1	How to Make a MN Will (2E)	$16.95	____

NEW YORK TITLES

Qty	ISBN	Title	Retail	Ext.
____	1-57248-193-5	Child Custody, Visitation and Support in NY	$26.95	____
____	1-57248-141-2	How to File for Divorce in NY (2E)	$26.95	____
____	1-57248-249-4	How to Form a Corporation in NY (2E)	$24.95	____
____	1-57248-095-5	How to Make a NY Will (2E)	$16.95	____
____	1-57248-199-4	How to Start a Business in NY (2E)	$18.95	____
____	1-57248-198-6	How to Win in Small Claims Court in NY (2E)	$18.95	____
____	1-57248-197-8	Landlords' Legal Guide in NY	$24.95	____
____	1-57071-188-7	New York Power of Attorney Handbook	$19.95	____
____	1-57248-122-6	Tenants' Rights in NY	$21.95	____

NEW JERSEY TITLES

Qty	ISBN	Title	Retail	Ext.
____	1-57248-239-7	How to File for Divorce in NJ	$24.95	____

NORTH CAROLINA TITLES

Qty	ISBN	Title	Retail	Ext.
____	1-57248-185-4	How to File for Divorce in NC (3E)	$22.95	____
____	1-57248-129-3	How to Make a NC Will (3E)	$16.95	____
____	1-57248-184-6	How to Start a Business in NC (3E)	$18.95	____
____	1-57248-091-2	Landlords' Rights & Duties in NC	$21.95	____

OHIO TITLES

Qty	ISBN	Title	Retail	Ext.
____	1-57248-190-0	How to File for Divorce in OH (2E)	$24.95	____
____	1-57248-174-9	How to Form a Corporation in OH	$24.95	____
____	1-57248-173-0	How to Make an OH Will	$16.95	____

PENNSYLVANIA TITLES

Qty	ISBN	Title	Retail	Ext.
____	1-57248-242-7	Child Custody, Visitation and Support in Pennsylvania	$26.95	____
____	1-57248-211-7	How to File for Divorce in PA (3E)	$26.95	____
____	1-57248-094-7	How to Make a PA Will (2E)	$16.95	____
____	1-57248-112-9	How to Start a Business in PA (2E)	$18.95	____
____	1-57248-245-1	The Landlord's Legal Guide in PA	$24.95	____

TEXAS TITLES

Qty	ISBN	Title	Retail	Ext.
____	1-57248-171-4	Child Custody, Visitation, and Support in TX	$22.95	____
____	1-57248-172-2	How to File for Divorce in TX (3E)	$24.95	____
____	1-57248-114-5	How to Form a Corporation in TX (2E)	$24.95	____
____	1-57248-255-9	How to Make a TX Will (3E)	$16.95	____
____	1-57248-214-1	How to Probate and Settle an Estate in TX (3E)	$26.95	____
____	1-57248-228-1	How to Start a Business in TX (3E)	$18.95	____
____	1-57248-111-0	How to Win in Small Claims Court in TX (2E)	$16.95	____
____	1-57248-110-2	Landlords' Rights and Duties in TX (2E)	$21.95	____

SUBTOTAL THIS PAGE ____

SUBTOTAL PREVIOUS PAGE ____

Shipping — $5.00 for 1st book, $1.00 each additional ____

Illinois residents add 6.75% sales tax ____

Connecticut residents add 6.00% sales tax ____

TOTAL ____

To order, call Sourcebooks at 1-800-432-7444 or FAX (630) 961-2168 (Bookstores, libraries, wholesalers—please call for discount)
Prices are subject to change without notice.
Find more legal information at: www.SphinxLegal.com